WESLEY AVILA
WITH RICHARD PARKS III

GUERRILLA TACOS

Recipes from the
Streets of L.A.

PHOTOGRAPHS BY DYLAN JAMES HO + JENI AFUSO
ILLUSTRATIONS BY MICHAEL HIRSHON
COVER GRAFFITI BY VYAL REYES

TEN SPEED PRESS
California | New York

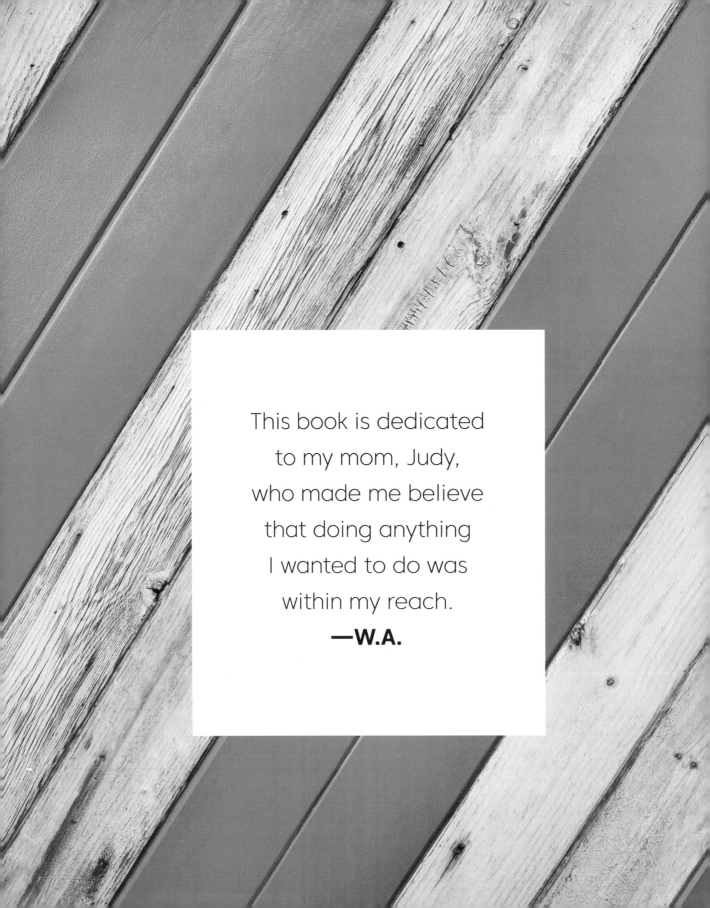

This book is dedicated
to my mom, Judy,
who made me believe
that doing anything
I wanted to do was
within my reach.

—W.A.

VI GUERRILLA FOOD STYLE 190

SALSAS

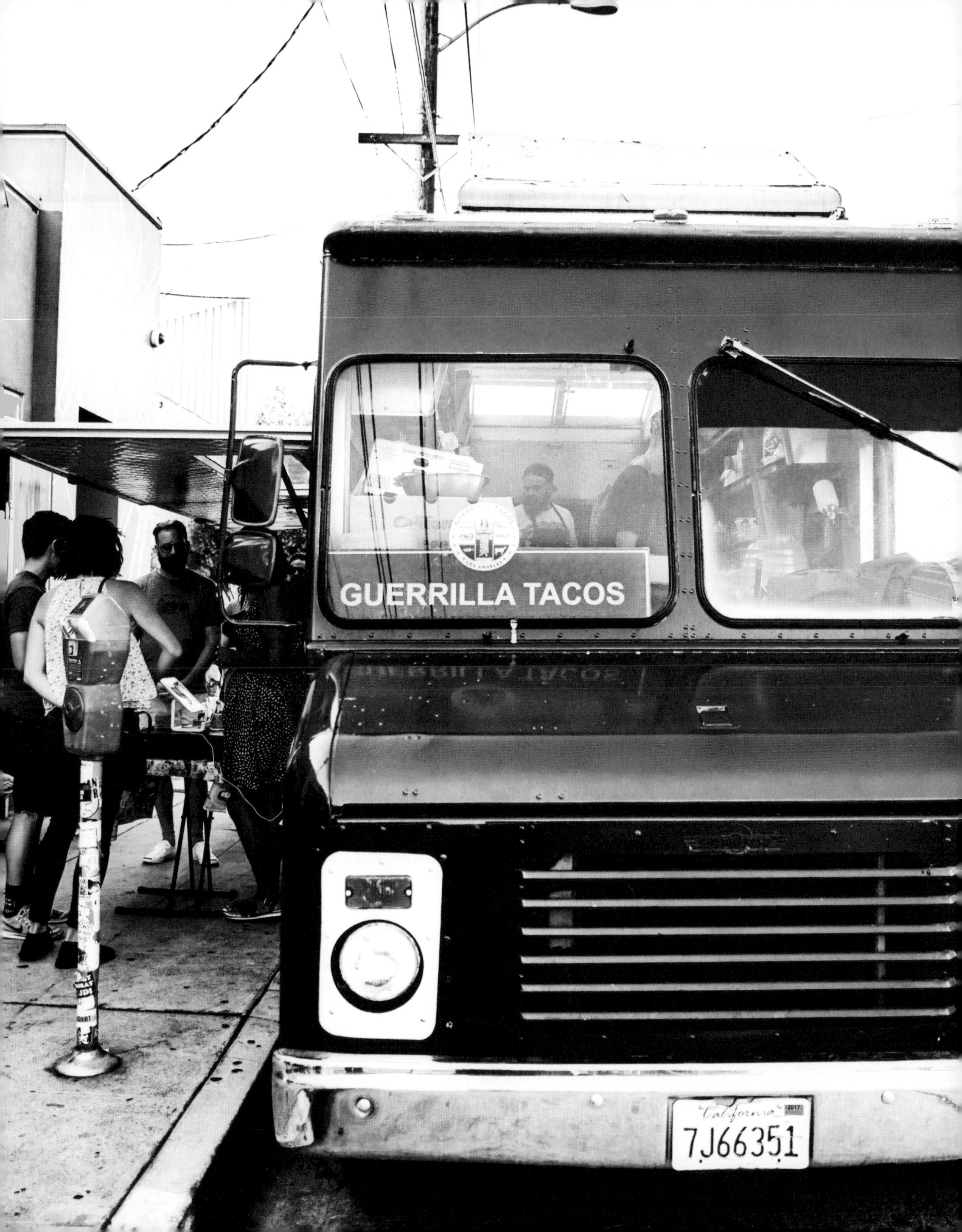
GUERRILLA TACOS
California
7J66351

I

AN INTRODUCTION TO

GUERRILLA TACOS

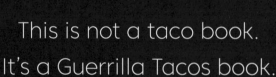

This is not a taco book.

It's a Guerrilla Tacos book.

THE RECIPES YOU FIND HERE WILL GIVE YOU ALL YOU NEED TO MAKE THE FOOD FROM GUERRILLA TACOS AT HOME TONIGHT. I DON'T PRETEND THERE'S ANY DEEP DARK SECRET TO WHAT I'M DOING. EVERYTHING IS PRESENTED IN AS STRAIGHTFORWARD A WAY AS POSSIBLE—A MIX OF FLAVORS AND TEXTURES AND COLORS PILED ONTO A FIVE-INCH TORTILLA AND SERVED ON A SMALL PAPER TRAY. WE MAKE PRETTY SIMPLE FOOD. BUT WE DO IT OUR OWN WAY.

What is a taco?

To me it's a tortilla and whatever you can dream up to put on top. Savory or sweet, stewed or grilled, soft or crispy, corn or flour—you can take it in any direction, as long as you can reasonably eat it with your hands. You can even put schwarma on a tortilla and call that a taco. I haven't done that, but now that I mention it, it doesn't sound half bad. Maybe I'll even try it at the truck next week.

What is Guerrilla Tacos?

It's all the flavors and food I dream about, usually on a tortilla. It's also the name of a food truck that parks in front of some of L.A.'s better coffee shops. Soon after this writing, it will become a brick-and-mortar restaurant. My wife, Tanya, came up with the name "guerrilla" because in the beginning, we were always in danger of being shut down by the cops. "You're like a guerrilla soldier, you do it your way, underground," she said to me. Sometimes it seems our lives resemble that of soldiers participating in unconventional warfare. With the truck, our locations, and with our tacos, everything is always changing, every single day. We keep it small, dynamic, guerrilla.

This is not "authentic" Mexican food. It's personal. I couldn't give a shit about authenticity, especially when it comes to tacos. A taco isn't just asada, pastor, and carnitas, with chopped onions and cilantro and your choice of salsa. The truth is there is no such thing as an authentic taco. Taco makers have always known this; if you look at the taqueros cooking in Mexico, there is always experimentation and a lot of "inauthentic" food. That's the tradition I see myself as a part of—the tradition of inauthenticity. Of not being a slave to tradition. Of experimenting. Evolving.

A taco is a blank canvas. How do you want to paint it? Let your imagination run wild. Seared cauliflower with raisins; tuna poke with furikake, uni, and habanero; Armenian beef basturma with a fried farm egg and burnt tomato salsa . . . corn tortillas go with everything. I consider anything an authentic Guerrilla Taco as long as I'm being authentic to myself and my perspective and experiences as a cook. *

Who am I? A fat kid from Pico Rivera, turned DJ, turned teamster, turned fine-dining cook, turned DIY food-truck chef. I am sleeved in tattoos and I have a season-pass to Disneyland. I love my wife and my dog and my family. And I love what I cook. The story of Guerrilla Tacos is also my story, told one taco at a time.

It's the story of my childhood in Pico where the house would fill with the aroma that came when my mother fried ground beef in lard with Lawry's taco seasoning on the stove top. It's a trip to Baja with my dad, where I tasted my first lobster, and to his hometown in a rural part of Durango, Mexico, where I sampled the most amazing wild anise. It's a mind-blowing tapas bar in Spain that serves nothing but wine and different kinds of mushrooms. It's learning the basics at culinary school, getting my fine-dining chops at L'Auberge Carmel with Walter Manzke, and slanging prime rib and liver and onions at a country club in Pacific Palisades.

I started Guerrilla Tacos on a whim in 2012 with a $300 cart I found in downtown L.A. and a hibachi grill. Only two kinds of tacos were served that day—chicken and steak. I had no idea what the following morning would bring. Since then, everything has changed. But I still can't tell you what's going to happen tomorrow.

In the few years since Guerrilla Tacos opened, I've gotten shingles from stress, been shut down by the police, and landed near the top of Jonathan Gold's best restaurants list—and the crazy thing is, we still don't even *have* a restaurant. Guerrilla Tacos is still very young. As we write this book, we're looking to open our first brick-and-mortar restaurant with a real grill and an open fire, things that weren't available at first as I cooked out of the cart or now out of the kitchen of the food truck. And soon, the truck will go away and Guerrilla Tacos will change into something new.

So this book is a snapshot of my cooking at a moment in time, and it is the story of how I got here, told through my life in food. As I have from day one, I'm going to keep moving from here, keep evolving, keep doing it guerrilla style.

PICO RIVERA

My mom's cooking, the best burrito on the planet, being a DJ, and leaving home.

PIO PICO ROAD RUNNERS
"CALVARY CHAPEL"
PICO RIVERA
WED.7PM SUN 8:15 IO 12:30
562 777-5134

THE SMELL OF MY MOTHER'S COOKING WAS ALWAYS IN THE AIR AT OUR HOUSE IN PICO RIVERA. PICO IS BASICALLY A SMALL CITY LOCATED SOUTHEAST OF DOWNTOWN LOS ANGELES, BUT IT'S ACTUALLY ITS OWN INCORPORATED CITY, WHERE NINE OUT OF EVERY TEN RESIDENTS ARE HISPANIC.

Julia Luz Alicia Ponce Avila, a.k.a. Judy (my mom), worked most of her life at a factory for Avery Labels, an office supply manufacturer in Whittier. She was a hard worker, but when she was off work, she was like Tracy Turnblad's friend from *Hairspray*—into deep cuts and good food. And today, I'm just like her. Deep cuts and good food. What else do you need?

Every day there was something different to eat—tightly rolled fried potato tacos with bright, fresh tomatillo salsa; braised meat and canned gravy with mashed potatoes and Bisquick or Pillsbury biscuits; ground beef tacos fried in the skillet in lard with Lawry's seasoning; albondigas; chile rellenos. Stuff that's just undeniably delicious and flavorful and hearty. No wonder I was such a fat kid, obsessed with food and eating. My favorite place to sit in that house in Pico was on the couch in the living room, taking in the sounds and smells of my mother's cooking in the next room.

Even when my mom was sick she still cooked for us; simple things like barbecued chicken or carnitas she picked up at the market. You'll see recipes from my mother in this book or if you come eat at my truck. There's always an homage to her in the food I cook, mostly because her cooking was just fucking good, and it's still the food I love to this day. The one recipe of my mother's that you won't see is tortas de calabasa (pumpkin tortas)—those I feared. Giant, horrible things, like dumplings but bigger, and tomato-y, and gnarly. I refused to eat them.

If we weren't eating food cooked at home by my mom or food from McDonald's, we would eat at Tonia's, the local spot in Pico Rivera that served my favorite burrito on the planet. Tonia's was a beacon, a humble shack churning out perfect food at the center of the neighborhood. Like a church or high school or rec center, there was Tonia's, serving home-style Mexican food to the hungry residents of Pico Rivera. "Tonia's Mexican food," the sign read in bright red and black typeface and "11 kinds of burritos." It was basically a walk-up counter with a few small tables outside. Posters of old-timey Mexican movie stars hung on the wall inside alongside plaques from local sports leagues. Tonia's fed our hunger for pozole and flautas

Tonia's was run by the Zaragoza family. Pico residents themselves, they took care of the neighborhood in return for our loyal support of the business. The employees didn't even turn away panhandlers, and I read somewhere they would take whatever change local bums happened to have in exchange for a hot meal and a cold drink. That's hospitality, because even if a guy's a little short on money, he wants to spend his dollar on you. You always have to remember that as a chef.

The state closed down Tonia's last year over a back taxes issue, and I have to say, that's just some bullshit and a real shame. Some creep from the Board of Equalization must have holed up in the alleyway off Rosemead near Beverly Boulevard behind Tonia's and started counting how many $2.95 burritos they were selling, how many customers were coming through, how many cups of fountain soda were going out of the walk-up counter. In the end, the state hit the Zaragoza family with a $300K bill, which, of course, they couldn't pay. Pico lost a little bit of its soul the day Tonia's closed.

But that burrito—oh, that burrito. Flour tortilla, warmed on the comal to stretchy, crispy perfection and filled with scoops of braised chicharrones. I am not talking about chicharrones you see in gas station rest stops by the way—those petrified, dried wagon wheel–looking pieces of overpriced salt. No. The chicharrones in the Tonia's burrito were gooey, like gummy bears left in the sun to melt into a delightful goopy mess, with an unmistakable, deep sienna color that is shared only by Mustang GTs of a certain vintage. They were served with chopped tomatoes and iceberg lettuce, which, while slightly beside the point, were still very much key ingredients to the most perfect burrito I've ever eaten.

I probably ate more often at Tonia's after my mom passed. It was a pretty quick downhill slide for my mom. I guess she had been sick for about three years when she died. Most of her adult life—fifteen years—she had spent working at that Avery Labels factory and cooking meals for us kids and our dad. She'd punch out at the factory in Whittier at night and come back to our house in Pico Rivera, where she'd cook us dinner, get us to bed, wake up, make us breakfast, get us to school, and then go back to the factory. Factory, home, dinner, bed, breakfast, factory. Repeat.

They make glue at the Avery factory for all the labels and office supplies they sell. One day my mom started coughing. The fumes got to her, I guess. We always thought she'd get better. Why was she coughing? We were kids; we couldn't figure it out. After a while she started losing weight. Then she stopped working. She was too weak.

And she couldn't stop coughing. It just snowballed. We still hoped that she might get better, but after a while, hope was all it was. Toward the end, my dad was driving her to doctors in L.A. and even down to Mexico for witchcraft. Nothing helped.

My mom never missed one of my football games. She bought me my first turntable set and mixer. And when I started working as a DJ, she'd drop me at house parties and pick me up late at night when I was done. I was fourteen or fifteen then, playing at a lot of parties in the East L.A./San Gabriel Valley scene. Even though she was sick, she was always happy to give me a ride home. I'd just page her when I was ready to go, and she'd turn up an hour later in her minivan. Whether it was a house party or a playoff game, my mother was there supporting my passions. Even when she was on oxygen toward the end of her life, she still made it to all my games and picked me up late from practice.

Football was my true passion. And I excelled at it. I was the captain of the team. In fact, I never thought success, in any field, was beyond reach for me. My mom has everything to do with that.

Life is awesome, and life fucking sucks. It just keeps going. Only in hindsight do I see that everything changed when my mom died. Before she passed, I was focused on being an athlete and a do-gooder. No smoking, no drinking. I was captain of the football team. But I went from being captain the year before she died to quitting the team the next year. I'd never seen such disappointment on my father's face as when I told him that I wasn't playing football my senior year. He was so pissed. I don't know exactly why I let it go but obviously I was grieving.

Without football, I didn't have any one thing to focus on. I wasn't much into school and since I wasn't involved in sports anymore, there wasn't much keeping me in class. I'd come in late, at lunchtime, or leave early, or ditch school entirely. I distanced myself from my old friends without realizing really why. My teachers knew I was going through some shit—they knew my mom had died, so they let a lot of stuff slide. They were like, "Just show up to class, and you'll pass." I kept up the facade of going to school, but really I was in a prolonged state of mourning.

By the time my mother died I had discovered girls, and after her death, I got unhealthily involved with my girlfriend at the time. Like, you probably should not have a girlfriend that is living with you when you are fifteen, but I basically did. My dad didn't know about it, of course. It's reasonable that he did not notice. He had just lost his wife and was raising three kids on his own and keeping it together at his job to provide for us. Plus, I was a conniving teenager whose world had just been shocked to the core. Girls/my girlfriend gave me a place to focus my energies.

My brother, sister, and I became latchkey kids. My dad worked long hours at a packing and shipping facility in Sante Fe Springs as a teamster. For a few weeks following my mom's death, my aunts came over with food, but then it tapered off and eventually stopped entirely.

My dad would sometimes cook for us after mom died. A lot of times he made breakfast for dinner—eggs and beans with panela cheese—or he made bistek. My dad's actually a good cook. I still make the Chubbs Taco (page 34) in his honor; nobody makes menudo—the famous Mexican tripe stew—like his. That soup is one of the highlights of my year, to this day. But at the same time, it was no replacement for my mom's cooking, not to mention, my mom herself.

It became super-quiet around the house, which was just strange. My brother, Jose, was working at a pizza place at the mall and had unlimited free pizza, which, as a teenager, is incredible. I started setting up my turntables in the living room of our house after school, and Jose would bring home free pizzas after his shift. From then on, it was just pizza and hip-hop at the house, *every single day*. Friends would come through for free pizza or to play records. It was fun, but mostly it was just passing the time. I also DJed house parties in the San Gabriel Valley and the like, but I wasn't ready to get a serious job, yet.

I was depressed, and I mourned my mother for a long time. It affects me to this day. I've learned that even now, I'm always waiting for the other shoe to drop. When's the next tragedy coming, the next big challenge? That's always on my mind. With the truck and Guerrilla Tacos, in general, I'm always waiting for something to happen.

About five years after mom's death, a class action lawsuit against Avery was settled, and each of us kids got about $9,000. With that money, I moved out of the house in Pico shortly after my twenty-first birthday.

TORTILLAS: A GUIDE

Our guide to buying and a master method for heating them up

PURCHASING QUALITY TORTILLAS

We're using 5-inch corn tortillas, unless otherwise noted. If you are in the area, get your tortillas from La Princesita in Boyle Heights (2426 E 4th St.) or in East L.A. (3432 E Cesar Chavez Ave.). When you Google, it sometimes shows up as La Princesa. La Princesita also has bomb-ass flour tortillas. Or if you want to spend a little bit more, go to Kernel of Truth Organics (kerneloftruthorganics.com), which sells organic non-GMO heritage corn tortillas made in Boyle Heights by Mexican guys. The corn they use is unbleached and a more natural product. If you don't live in L.A., try to get some kind of local tortilla. Just look for the tortilla that uses the best possible ingredients. Mass-produced tortillas are awful. They use the entire corn cob instead of just the kernels. It makes brittle and flavorless tortillas. Please don't use those. Look at the ingredients list. You're looking for tortillas that are made from corn, water, and lime (calcium hydroxide), but nothing else. We occasionally use flour tortillas, and those you should also get from La Princesita or else try to find a local option. The same rules apply for flour tortillas as for corn.

HEATING TORTILLAS

In a cast-iron skillet, or on a griddle, over medium heat, warm a knob of unsalted butter (½ to 1 tablespoon). Add tortillas one at a time. Coat the first side with the melted butter and then immediately flip to coat the second side. Season with a little salt. Don't crisp or brown them, but if you're in danger of doing so, flip them over and let them heat until warm. Repeat in batches until you have enough tortillas to serve. If you're keeping the heat at medium and your pan is clean and well-seasoned, you should be fine; just watch out for burning and browning!

If you're working in batches, put the warmed tortillas into a plastic container lined with paper towels. Just stack on top of each other. Once you've heated them all, keep them warm by covering with another towel and closing the lid until you are ready to use them. They'll stay warm for about 10 minutes.

SWEET POTATO TACO

After my mom passed away, my aunt used to make us tons of *tacos de papa dorados*—basically mashed potatoes inside a tortilla either folded or rolled up like a flauta and fried—and leave them in big bags in the fridge. My friends and I would grab a few, microwave them, smother them in tart, fresh, bright-green tomatillo salsa, and wolf them down while watching episodes of Richard Bey. It's a *casero*-style (homemade) snack, sort of like a Hot Pocket. You wouldn't really see these on a menu anywhere. So when I first got the cart, I figured why not make this taco with a few modifications.

The idea here is comfort—a little sweet from the potatoes, a little tart from the French feta, some crunch from the fried corn, and some heat from the salsa. The salsa isn't a Mexican thing, it's a Spanish thing, like a romesco with added spice from the habanero and chiles de árbol. At first we were doing this with Oaxacan melted cheese and braised leeks, but we don't have the time and space to braise leeks so we add the fresh scallions instead. I like a lot of onion on my tacos. These days you can probably get something like this at other places, but back when we started out, you would never see sweet potato on a taco. Other things cycle in and out seasonally but this is on the menu year-round because it is our best-selling taco.

3 pounds sweet potatoes (Japanese sweet potatoes are best, the long and thin kind with the red skin), skins on

Kosher salt

Almond Salsa

1 tablespoon lard or canola oil

½ cup loose-packed dried, stemmed, and roughly torn dried chiles de árbol

6 garlic cloves, peeled

3 tablespoons slivered almonds

1 pound tomatillos, husked and rinsed

1 cup rough-chopped store-bought roasted red bell peppers

½ cup water

Kosher salt

In a large saucepan or 6-quart stockpot, combine the sweet potatoes and enough cold water to cover. Add salt until it's as salty as the sea. Set over high heat and bring to a boil, then turn the heat to a gentle simmer. Simmer the potatoes until they're just cooked—you can stick a knife into one and it comes out clean—about 12 minutes. Drain and set the potatoes aside. When they're cool enough to handle, slice them into ¾-inch coins or bite-size pieces and set aside.

To make the almond salsa: While the potatoes are simmering, warm a cast-iron skillet over medium-low heat. When the pan is hot, add the lard. Once the lard is melted, add the chiles de árbol. When the chiles are browned all over and smelling toasty, add the garlic and almonds and cook for 30 seconds. Don't burn the garlic! Burnt garlic is the worst. When the garlic is slightly golden brown, add the tomatillos, roasted peppers, water, and 1 teaspoon salt to the pan.

continued

Cover and cook until the tomatillos are mushy, about 8 minutes—they should split easily and break apart when you push them with a spoon.

Remove the skillet from the heat and, using a slotted spoon, transfer the solid ingredients to a blender and reserve the cooking liquid in the pan. Add the olive oil, red wine vinegar, and habanero to the blender. Cover the blender well and watch out you don't touch the hot chile seeds during this part. Blend until the salsa is nice and smooth, and then season with salt. You want a little acidity, plus the sweetness from the roasted peppers and heat from the habanero and chiles de árbol. Check the salsa and add some of the leftover cooking liquid to reach your desired consistency. It should be almost as thick as a milk shake.

Put your largest cast-iron skillet over medium-high heat and warm the butter until it's melted and bubbling but not burning. Add a layer of the potatoes to the pan—you want both sides of each potato slice to get a little browned, but not tough or crispy. Add some of the thyme and cook the potatoes until golden brown, about 15 minutes. Flip them and brown the other side. Set the browned potatoes aside on a plate and cover with foil to keep them warm. Repeat until all the sweet potatoes are browned, using more butter as needed.

On top of each tortilla, add, in this order, three or four slices of potato, 1 tablespoon salsa, 1 tablespoon feta, ½ tablespoon corn nuts, and a sprinkle of scallions. Serve immediately.

3 tablespoons extra-virgin olive oil

2 teaspoons red wine vinegar

1 dried habanero chile (use half if you don't like your salsa too spicy), stemmed

2 tablespoons unsalted butter, plus more as needed

3 thyme sprigs

8 corn tortillas, warmed (see page 29)

4 ounces feta cheese (Valbreso if you can find it), crumbled

4 tablespoons corn nuts

1 bunch of scallions, green parts only, sliced about ⅛ inch thick (reserve the white parts for something else)

CHUBBS TACO

This is my dad's taco, something he'd cook up for us fast, in the months after my mom passed away. For lunch, for dinner, whenever. It's hearty, filling, rich, and full of protein. My dad's fried egg is something I've never seen before or since—fried in the skillet in about an inch of lard, so the eggs just float on top. The eggs puff up and get the color of a chile relleno. It's like a deflated Yorkshire Pudding or an egg pancake. I was always a fat kid. "Are you going to eat twenty tacos?" my dad used to ask me in Spanish. It was a joke, but not mean-spirited. It was always with *cariño*—with love. He always called me chubby, so I started calling him Chubbs.

Whenever we make this taco at the truck, people don't know what to say. It's not like anything you can get anywhere else.

2 cups dried pinto beans

1 yellow onion, quartered

2 bay leaves

1 head of garlic, halved lengthwise

Kosher salt

Arbol Salsa

½ cup dried chiles de árbol

2 to 3 tablespoons vegetable oil

1 teaspoon cumin seeds

2 cups tomatillos, husked and rinsed

6 garlic cloves, peeled and halved

¼ cup water

Kosher salt

¼ cup white vinegar

4 eggs

1 red or white onion, minced very fine, as fine as possible, like rice or smaller

½ teaspoon kosher salt

½ cup lard

Rinse the pinto beans and discard any imperfect ones or small stones. Put the beans in a pot, cover with water, and place over medium heat until they're bubbling. Add the onion, bay leaves, and garlic and simmer slowly. Don't salt your beans until they're done; otherwise it will extract the water from the beans and you want them to absorb the water. When the beans are cooked and break apart when pressed with a spoon, remove them from the heat and season with salt. Set aside to steep.

To make the arbol salsa: While the beans cook, put the chiles de árbol in a 10-inch cast-iron skillet with 1 tablespoon of the vegetable oil. Get those nice and toasty; if it's getting hard to breathe in the house, you're doing it right. Maybe you're coughing a bit. Add the cumin seeds and cook for 2 minutes, but do not let them burn. Add the tomatillos and garlic. Add another 1 tablespoon oil; you're not going to taste it, but you want to coat the tomatillos, so maybe add the remaining 1 tablespoon oil. Roast the tomatillos enough to get a little color on them and then add the water so they don't burn. Cook over low to medium-high heat for 10 to 12 minutes, or until the tomatillos are squishy and completely soft. Using a slotted spoon, transfer the solid ingredients to a blender and blend on high speed until thoroughly mixed. Season with salt and add the vinegar. This can be done

continued

continued // CHUBBS TACO

A handful of pork cracklings
(see Box, opposite) or chicharrones
from the *carniceria* (butcher shop)

4 corn tortillas, warmed
(see page 29)

6 ounces queso fresco, broken
up or sliced (do not substitute
crumbly-ass cheese like *cotija*,
you want that fresh cooling to
counter the eggs)

½ avocado, pitted, peeled,
quartered, and very thinly sliced

4 dried chiles de árbol

Chopped chives for garnishing

ahead of time; if you're doing it more than a half day ahead,
transfer to an airtight container and store in the fridge.

Line a plate with paper towels.

Crack the eggs into a bowl. Add the onion and scramble it up with
the eggs. You don't want to scramble these eggs in the pan, that's
not how we cook them, so make sure they are good and scrambled
before hitting the lard. Add the salt and keep scrambling.

In a skillet over medium heat, melt the lard. (I wouldn't use anything
else but lard here. Butter might be good, but I like it with lard. My
dad always used lard, probably because it was super-cheap.) Add
one-fourth of the beaten eggs to the skillet. *Don't touch them!*—
just let them do their thing; these tacos are made to order. When
you think the eggs are cooked, cook them a little longer. You want
them golden brown, like a chile relleno, or the color the edges
of an egg get when you fry it in the pan normally. You don't want
them yellow. Don't worry about the eggs getting bitter. When
you can, look underneath and see that color, about 2½ minutes,
then use the biggest spatula you have (or two) to flip the eggs
over. Don't worry if the edges get messed up when you flip them.

Baste the eggs a bit with the lard, and add one-fourth of the cracklings as you baste, so they heat up with the eggs. Maybe some get mixed in with the eggs. When the eggs are fully brown and puffy, take your egg pancake out of the pan and let it drain on the prepared plate. Repeat the process for the three other tacos.

Remove the bay leaf, onion, and garlic from the bean pot. Discard all but 2 tablespoons of the lard from the skillet you used for the eggs and set over medium heat. Using a large slotted spoon, put about 1 cup of beans in the pan and, with the back of the spoon, smash your beans. Add some of the broth from the beans to thin the beans out a bit, until it's about the consistency of hummus. (If you have leftover whole beans, keep them in the fridge and eat with every meal, like a true Angeleno, until all the beans are gone.)

Spread 2 tablespoons of the beans onto each tortilla; then an egg, some cheese, avocado, and chiles de árbol; and sprinkle some chives on top. Serve immediately.

PORK CRACKLINGS

I advise buying pork cracklings at the store, preferably chicharrones from the Mexican *carniceria* (butcher shop) if you can. Otherwise, buy about 2 pounds of salt pork or pork belly and braise it in lard on the stove top for 3 hours. Just bring the heat to medium-low and simmer the pork for a long time, until the meat becomes very crispy. Let it go until it's golden brown. Chop up into small pieces using a chef's knife. Those are your pork cracklings. You can leave these out on the counter for 2 days. Eat them with the leftover beans.

POCHO TACO

Pocho is a slang term for a person of Mexican descent who's born in the States. My mom fried these tacos with lard. This is the "Taco Tuesday" taco. This is the hard-shelled taco like at Tito's in West L.A. Okay, maybe you haven't heard of Tito's, so I'll say it—it's like the Taco Bell hard-shelled taco. The taco-emoji taco. Well, my version anyway. But there's no shredded lettuce. I like shredded lettuce on other people's tacos. But not on my tacos! Do as I say, not as I do, I guess. Oh and I hate cotija cheese! It smells like feet. No cotija cheese in this taco, or in this book. You're going to need 24 wooden clothespins soaked in water for about 45 minutes to hold the tacos closed while frying.

This is something you'd make when you have a large group coming over.

Lemon Crema

2 cups crème fraîche or sour cream

¼ cup minced shallots

¼ cup minced fresh chives

Zest and juice of 2 Meyer or regular lemons

Burnt Tomato Salsa

8 Roma tomatoes

1 serrano chile, stemmed

1 jalapeño chile, stemmed

½ red onion

6 garlic cloves

¼ cup white vinegar

Kosher salt

3 cups peeled and cubed russet potatoes

Kosher salt

To make the lemon crema: In a large bowl, combine the crème fraîche, shallots, chives, and lemon zest and juice and whisk vigorously. The consistency should be the same as sour cream. Set aside.

To make the burnt tomato salsa: In a 10-inch cast-iron skillet over medium-high heat, cook the tomatoes until they are black on the bottom. Like black-black, almost to the point where they're getting gray, about 35 minutes. Flip them as you go so they blacken on all sides evenly.

In a food processor, combine the tomatoes, serrano, jalapeño, red onion, garlic, and vinegar. Pulse, but keep it chunky and leave the seeds and the charred bits in there. Season with salt. Set aside.

Add the cubed potatoes to a stockpot and cover them with cold water. Bring to a boil and then lower the heat to a simmer. Add 2 tablespoons salt and simmer until the potatoes are soft, about 15 minutes. Remove one and cut into it with a knife. It should be easy to pierce.

continued

In a 12-inch cast-iron skillet over medium heat, warm the vegetable oil. Add the meat and let brown, breaking it up with a wooden spoon as you go. Season with salt. Using a slotted spoon, transfer the meat to a plate but leave the fat in the pan.

Add the shallots, onion, and pequins to the rendered fat in the skillet and sauté over medium heat until the onion is translucent, about 3 minutes. Then add the potatoes, cumin, garlic powder, and onion powder; stir; and cook for another 3 to 5 minutes, until the potatoes have a little bit of color on them. Add the pine nuts and cook until crispy but not burnt, about 2 minutes. Remove the pan from the heat and stir in the meat and fully mix.

Spoon some meat and potatoes—3 or 4 tablespoons per taco—into each tortilla. Don't be cheap with the meat, but make sure the taco can close on itself. Use a soaked clothespin to hold the taco together for frying (see photo, page 39). Set aside. Repeat with the remaining tortillas until the filling is gone.

In a 10-inch cast-iron skillet over high heat, warm 1 cup vegetable oil, or enough to cover the tacos three-fourths of the way up the sides when they're lying flat. Line a plate or baking sheet with paper towels.

Bring the oil's temperature to about 360°F. Using tongs, add as many tacos as you can without crowding the pan, and fry until golden brown, about 2 minutes per side. Flip them with the tongs and fry the other side until golden brown. There will be bits floating around but don't trip. Use a spider or slotted spoon to get some out if they start burning. When the tacos are fried, remove them with the tongs and place on the prepared plate. Season with salt immediately. Repeat until all the tacos are fried.

Delicately open up each taco with your hands and add the cheddar so it's covering the meat, then some salsa, 2 tablespoons cubed tomato, and a dollop of crema. Serve immediately.

1 tablespoon vegetable oil

4 pounds ground boar meat or beef

½ cup minced shallots

1 cup finely diced yellow onion

3 dried pequin chiles, with seeds, stemmed and chopped

1½ teaspoons ground cumin

1 tablespoon garlic powder

1 tablespoon onion powder

½ cup pine nuts

24 corn tortillas, warmed (see page 29)

Vegetable oil for frying

1 pound yellow cheddar, shredded or rough chopped

2 cups cubed heirloom tomatoes or halved cherry tomatoes

FRIED BAJA TACO

Baja fish tacos are probably the second-most-popular taco you can get anywhere. Here we tried to re-create our version of a fish taco from one of the many stands in Ensenada, Baja California. We use cod in our recipe but in Baja they use locally caught mako or thresher shark. You can use any kind of good sustainable fish for this. *Do not* use farmed tilapia. We like Pacific mako, thresher, cod, pollock, and shrimp.

Cabbage Slaw

½ red cabbage, shredded very thinly, preferably with a mandoline

½ green cabbage, shredded very thinly, preferably with a mandoline

1 cup chopped fresh cilantro, plus ¾ cup rough-chopped cilantro stems

Juice of 4 limes

Kosher salt

Pico de Gallo Salsa

1 pound heirloom or Roma tomatoes, cored and chopped into ½-inch pieces

¼ red onion, minced

2 serrano chiles, stemmed and sliced very thin

½ cup chopped fresh cilantro

1 garlic clove, minced

Juice of 4 limes

Kosher salt

½ teaspoon freshly ground black pepper

Dijon Aïoli

1 tablespoon Dijon mustard

1 egg yolk

3 garlic cloves, peeled

2 white anchovies

To make the cabbage slaw: In a large bowl, combine both cabbages, the cilantro, cilantro stems, and lime juice; season with salt; and stir gently until mixed. Set aside.

To make the pico de gallo salsa: In a medium bowl, combine the tomatoes, onion, serranos, cilantro, garlic, and lime juice; season with salt and the pepper; and stir gently until mixed. Set aside.

To make the dijon aïoli: In a blender, combine the mustard, egg yolk, garlic, anchovies, lemon juice, Tabasco, Worcestershire, and shiso and blend on low-medium speed. Begin adding the vegetable oil slowly. Keep adding vegetable oil until you have a consistency thinner than mayo. Adjust the seasoning with salt and lemon juice. Transfer to an airtight container and keep in the fridge for up to 1 week.

To make the dijon crema: In a food processor, combine the sour cream, aïoli, chipotle in adobo, and the habanero and process until completely blended. Place in the fridge until you're ready to use.

Cut the fish into pieces about the size of your middle finger, or about 3 ounces each. Season with salt. Put 2 cups of the cornstarch into a small bowl. Dust the fish in the cornstarch until it's completely coated and then set aside.

Fill a Dutch oven over medium-high heat with about 3 inches of vegetable oil and bring to 365° to 375°F. (To test the heat, grab an extra tortilla. If when you dip the tortilla in the oil, it floats back up to the surface, it's good. If it fries or browns right up, lower the heat a little.) Set a wire rack over a baking sheet and place near the stove.

continued

Juice of 1 lemon, or as needed

9 dashes Tabasco sauce

4 dashes Worcestershire sauce

8 shiso leaves

1 cup vegetable oil

Kosher salt

Dijon Crema

1½ cups sour cream

1½ cups Dijon Aïoli (see above)

2 tablespoons chipotle in adobo

1 habanero chile, stemmed

3 pounds cod fillets, patted dry

Kosher salt

2½ cups cornstarch

Vegetable oil for frying, plus
1 tablespoon

1 cup all-purpose flour

1 teaspoon baking soda

1 teaspoon onion powder

1 teaspoon garlic powder

1 teaspoon paprika

One 12-ounce bottle pilsner beer

1 egg

1 teaspoon freshly ground
black pepper

12 dried chiles japones, stemmed
and toasted

12 corn tortillas, warmed
(see page 29)

4 limes, quartered (optional)

In a medium bowl, mix together the flour, baking soda, onion powder, garlic powder, paprika, and remaining ½ cup cornstarch. In a second bowl, mix together the beer and egg. Pour the dry ingredients into the beer mixture while whisking at a medium rate, just enough so the ingredients are incorporated into a batter. Season with salt and the pepper.

One at a time, submerge the cornstarch-dusted fish in the batter to fully coat it. Let some batter drip off and use the side of the bowl to wipe off any excess. You want the fish totally coated but not dripping. Dunk each piece halfway into the oil, swish it forward once about 6 inches, back in the other direction, and then drop it in. Don't crowd the pan too much or you'll lower the temperature. Using tongs, gently roll the pieces around and fry until golden brown. Using a slotted spoon, remove to the prepared rack, season with salt immediately. Repeat battering and frying the remaining fish. Let them dry slightly, but you want to serve them hot.

In a skillet over medium-high heat, warm the 1 tablespoon vegetable oil. Add the chiles japones and toss to coat in the oil. Cook until aromatic and the chiles change from crimson to crimson-brown, about 30 seconds. Using a slotted spoon, immediately remove from the heat and set aside.

Add 1 tablespoon crema, some fish, slaw, and pico de gallo to each tortilla. Break the toasted chiles over the top to add some flakey, smoky heat. Serve immediately, with the lime quarters, for diners to squeeze over the top, if desired.

B SIDE: **LITTLE SAIGON VERSION**

I like bahn mi. It occurred to me that the slaw you find on a bahn mi is similar to a Baja taco. This makes it a little funkier, a little sweeter, but just as good. Prepare the tacos as described but substitute this variation on the slaw.

To make the salsa bruja: In a mixing bowl, combine the fish sauce, lime juice, and sugar and whisk until the sugar is dissolved. Add the ginger, chiles, and garlic and mix until the chiles are completely coated. Transfer the salsa to a squeeze bottle—you just want to use the juice, not the chiles themselves.

In a separate bowl, combine the carrots, cucumber, bean sprouts, mint, peanuts, and sesame seeds. Add the salsa to taste (I'd probably use all of it) and stir to combine the slaw before using.

Salsa Bruja

½ cup fish sauce (I like Red Boat Fish Sauce)

½ cup fresh lime juice

1 tablespoon sugar

1 tablespoon grated fresh ginger

¼ cup very, very thinly sliced Thai bird, serrano, or habanero chiles

3 garlic cloves, sliced paper-thin

2 cups peeled and julienned carrots

2 cups peeled, seeded, and julienned cucumber

1 cup bean sprouts

2 cups torn fresh mint leaves

1 cup toasted peanuts

1 tablespoon toasted sesame seeds

LOBSTER TACO

When we would camp out in Rosarito Beach in Baja, California, back in the '80s, my dad and I would hike from our campground all the way to this place called Ortega's Restaurant, where we would eat lobster omelettes, lobster tacos, and poached lobster. You can get every kind of lobster you want at Ortega's, but it always comes with refried beans. When I eat buttery lobster with refried beans, it always reminds me of cloudy mornings in Baja, hiking with my dad at 7 a.m. Make the beans first—it takes about an hour and a half for them to cook. In the meantime, make the salsa and the lobster.

Wash the pinto beans and remove any imperfect ones or small stones. Place the beans in a pot, cover with water, and place over medium heat until they're bubbling. Add the onion, bay leaves, and garlic and simmer slowly. Don't salt your beans until they're done; otherwise it will extract the water from the beans and you want them to absorb the water. When the beans are cooked and break apart when pressed with a spoon, remove them from the heat and season with salt. Set aside to steep.

To make the roasted habanero-serrano salsa: While the beans cook, using a mesh grate or metal basket, roast all the chiles on the stove top over high heat until black. The habaneros will blacken quickly because of their sugars—pull them off first, and then the serranos. Or, you can use a cast-iron skillet for this; toss to blacken them evenly all over.

In a food processor, combine the blackened chiles and garlic. The garlic will cook a little bit with the heat of the roasted chiles, but hopefully not too much—you want that raw flavor. Pulse a few times, add the vinegar, and season with salt. Then blend on high speed—it should stay chunky and have a nice dark green and orange color with bits of blackened skin. Set aside.

Fill an 8-quart stockpot with water, bring to a boil, and add the ½ cup salt. When the water is boiling and the salt is dissolved, add the onion, carrots, celery, bay leaf, peppercorns, and lemon juice. Bring back to a boil.

continued

2 cups dried pinto beans

1 yellow onion, quartered

2 bay leaves

1 head of garlic, cut in half lengthwise

Kosher salt

Roasted Habanero-Serrano Salsa

6 habanero chiles, stemmed

8 serrano chiles, stemmed

6 garlic cloves, peeled

¼ cup white wine vinegar

Kosher salt

½ cup kosher salt

1 white onion, rough chopped

4 medium carrots, peeled and rough chopped

2 celery stalks, trimmed and rough chopped

1 bay leaf

6 peppercorns

Juice of 2 lemons

One 1½- to 2-pound live
Maine lobster

2 tablespoons lard

2 cups vegetable oil

1 cup flat-leaf parsley leaves,
torn from stems, washed, and
patted dry

¼ cup unsalted butter

6 garlic cloves, peeled
and minced

Four 5-inch flour tortillas, warmed
(see page 29)

3 limes, halved

¼ cup salted, roasted, shelled
pistachios

Meanwhile, using two kitchen towels, one in each hand, grab the
lobster's body with your left hand (and towel) and grab the tail
with your right and twist until it breaks from the body. Pierce the
small opening at the base of the tail with a 10-inch wooden or
metal skewer and run it up the length of the tail. Set aside.

Return to the lobster with the kitchen towels. Hold the body down
and twist at the base of the left knuckle—where it connects to the
body—to rip off the knuckle and claw as a piece. Repeat with
the right knuckle/claw. Discard the body, or reserve for another use.

Place all the lobster pieces on a wire rack set over a baking sheet
to drain excess fluid. Prepare an ice-water bath in the largest
mixing bowl you have by stirring together water and a tray of ice.

Set a timer for 6 minutes and drop the knuckles and claws into the
boiling water. After 2 minutes, drop in the tail. When the timer goes
off, using tongs, pull out all the lobster and dump into the ice-water
bath. When cooled, remove from the bath and set aside.

Remove the bay leaf, onion, and garlic from the bean pot. Add
the lard to a large skillet. Using a large slotted spoon, transfer the
beans to the skillet (do not discard bean water from pot!) and, with
the back of the spoon, smash your beans. Add some of the broth
from the beans to thin the beans out a bit, until they're about the
consistency of hummus.

Pour the vegetable oil into a cast-iron skillet over medium-high
heat. Throw in a parsley leaf to see that it's hot enough for frying—
it should sizzle immediately and start turning a brighter green—
and adjust the heat accordingly. Add all the parsley to the pan,
being careful not to crowd it. When the leaves are brighter and
getting crispy, remove with a slotted spoon and transfer to a clean
paper towel.

Using a kitchen towel, place the lobster in the palm of your hand
with the flesh side facing up, and squeeze the sides until the
shell cracks. Use both your thumbs to split the tail shell apart and
remove the meat to a cutting board. Twist the knuckles away from

continued

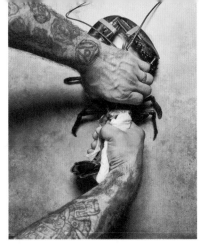

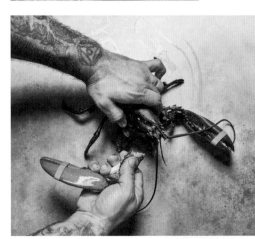

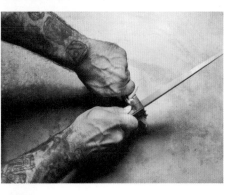

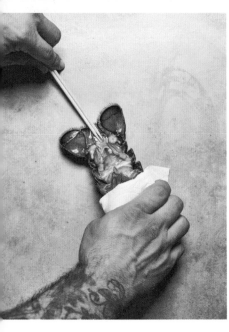

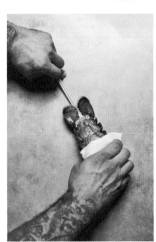

the claws. Hold the hilt of your knife to the seam of the knuckle and tap it onto a cutting board. Don't chop it off—wedge the knife into the seam, then move the blade side to side until the shell separates. Pull the claw meat out with your hands. Last, use kitchen shears to cut through the knuckle shell. Remove the knuckle meat and set aside.

In a large pan over medium heat, melt the butter. Add the garlic and sauté until aromatic, 15 seconds or so. Add the lobster and poach in the warm garlic butter for 2 to 3 minutes, until well-coated and slightly browned in places.

Add a smear of refried beans to each of the warmed tortillas, then add the lobster pieces. Squeeze some lime juice over that and top with salsa, fried parsley, and pistachios. Serve immediately.

GREEN BEAN AND EGG TACO

There are some combinations of food that remind me of specific times and meals in my life and are very strong emotional triggers. This one in particular is close to my heart. When I was a little kid, my mom would make scrambled eggs with green beans, which I thought was not very appealing. "Try it before you knock it," she told me. I did and I loved it. She used to make it with canned, gnarly green beans and scramble it with a little bit of lard and eggs. In this version I upped the ante and used seasonal baby green beans and elevated it a little bit with nicer ingredients.

This is one of the most comforting tacos that I make.

To make the red pepper escabeche: In a 4-quart saucepan over medium heat, combine the roasted peppers, garlic, thyme, sherry vinegar, olive oil, and 7-Up. Bring to a simmer, stirring occasionally, until the liquid is reduced by about half, about 20 minutes. You'll be left with a very seasoned oil and the peppers will have a very deep red color. Set aside. You'll want to serve them lukewarm.

Prepare an ice-water bath in the largest mixing bowl you have by stirring together water and a tray of ice.

Bring a large pot of water to a boil over high heat. Add the haricot verts and blanch for about 2 minutes, or until al dente. Using a slotted spoon, transfer the haricot verts to the ice-water bath to cool immediately so they don't overcook. Once cooled, place onto napkins to drain excess water completely.

In a large, cast-iron skillet over medium-high heat, melt 3 tablespoons of the butter. Add the garlic and thyme and cook until aromatic, about 10 seconds. Add the haricot verts and sauté for 2 minutes, until they're slightly blistered. Season with salt and pepper. Remove the garlic and thyme. Add the pine nuts and raisins and continue sautéing for 1 minute. Remove from the heat and zest the lemon on top and season with additional salt and pepper. Set aside.

continued

Red Pepper Escabeche

4 red bell peppers, roasted, skins removed, and left whole, or from a jar

4 garlic cloves, peeled and thinly sliced

4 thyme sprigs

½ cup sherry vinegar

½ cup extra-virgin olive oil

½ cup 7-Up or Sprite

2 pounds haricot verts or other baby green beans (yellow, purple), the skinnier and smaller, the better, stemmed

6 tablespoons unsalted butter

4 garlic cloves, peeled and smashed with side of a knife

2 thyme sprigs

Kosher salt

Freshly ground black pepper

¼ cup pine nuts

¼ cup golden raisins

1 lemon

Crack the eggs into a large bowl and lightly beat.

In a large, nonstick pan over medium-low heat, melt the remaining 3 tablespoons butter. Add the eggs and, using a rubber spatula, stir constantly so they're totally mixed and not sticking to the pan. When the eggs are still slightly runny, remove the pan from the heat and keep stirring. When the eggs are just set, leave them alone.

Place a portion of haricot verts onto each tortilla and add some soft scrambled egg. Use about 1 tablespoon escabeche to garnish each, breaking the peppers apart a bit, and top with some salsa and sprinkle with chives. Serve immediately.

12 eggs

12 corn tortillas, warmed (see page 29)

Arbol Salsa (page 34) for topping

Minced chives for garnishing

BREAKFAST BURRITO

A standard Mexican American breakfast burrito is chorizo and *pappas* (potatoes). It tends to be greasy and emulsified in fat. A lot of store-bought chorizo is super-soft, and when you put it in a pan over heat it just dissolves into lard. Like Carmelita's, the East L.A. brand I grew up on with the logo of a little pig holding a baseball bat. It comes in a tube. My mom would make us breakfast burritos with that, along with potatoes. Sometimes with eggs. It's like a hash, but super-fatty. The chorizo fat rendering off will turn your tortilla orange. It's the best kids' food. This is the adult version, using Cook Pig Ranch fatback. I want to open a quick pick-up place and serve just these breakfast burritos. This is the breakfast burrito to end all burritos.

6 large russet potatoes, peeled and cubed

8 quarts cold water, plus more as needed

3 tablespoons kosher salt

Chorizo

3 guajillo chiles

1 pound leaf lard or pork fat, cubed

1 pound pork cushion meat—shoulder or leg—ground

2 tablespoons kosher salt

3 tablespoons paprika

8 garlic cloves, minced

2 teaspoons freshly ground black pepper

2 teaspoons dried oregano

2 teaspoons ground cumin

1 teaspoon ground cloves

1 teaspoon ground coriander

2 tablespoons crushed chiles de árbol

½ cup distilled white vinegar

6 burrito-size flour tortillas

6 fried eggs (optional)

chopped chives (optional)

In a 12-quart stockpot, combine the potatoes and cold water. Set the pot over high heat. When the water is simmering, add the salt and cook until the potatoes are fork-tender, about 15 minutes. Drain in a colander and set the potatoes aside.

To make the chorizo: In a small saucepan over high heat, combine the guajillos with about an inch of water and let steep. When the guajillos are soft, remove them from the heat. When they are cool enough to handle, remove the seeds and the stem.

In a food processor, pulse the lard a few times, and then blend. Add the pork bit by bit until the pork and lard are ground very fine and take on a paté-like structure. It should be coarse but very spreadable. Add the salt, paprika, garlic, pepper, oregano, cumin, cloves, coriander, chiles, and vinegar, which should loosen the chorizo a bit. Use a rubber spatula to push any meat sticking to the sides back down and mix it again.

In a cast-iron skillet over medium-high heat, cook the chorizo and render off the fat. Add the potatoes and let them cook until they start to crust a bit on the bottom, about 6 minutes.

Warm the tortillas on a comal—just warm, not crispy. Assemble your burritos with as much chorizo as you like. Top with a fried egg and chives, if you'd like. You know they're right when the pork fat's dripping down your arm.

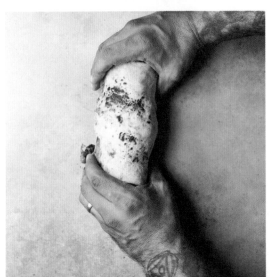

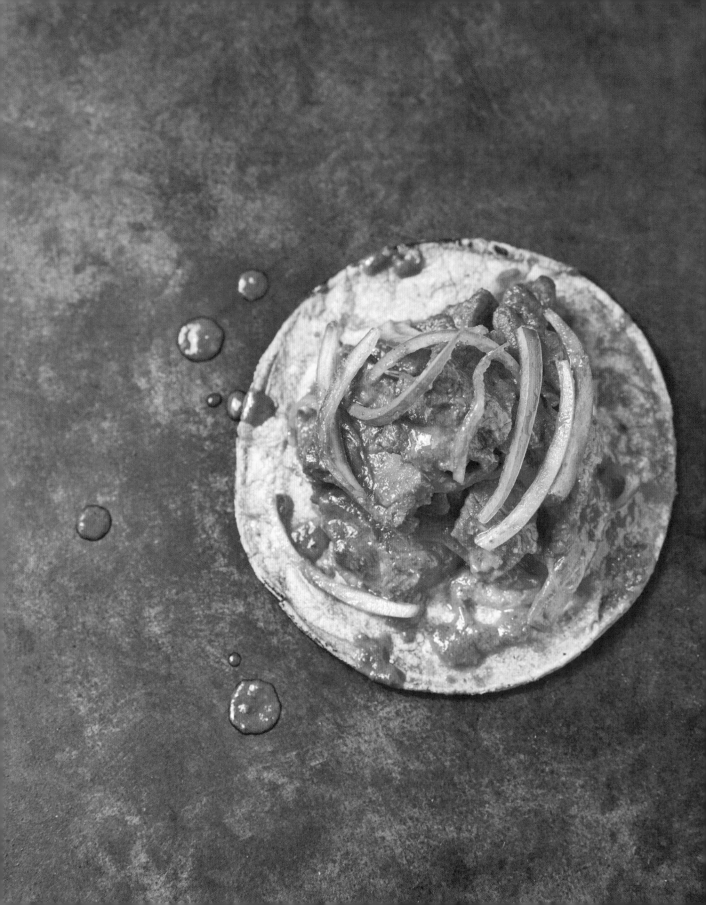

CHILE COLORADO

This is my dad's take on chile Colorado. He'd just make a simple *guisado* (stew) with sliced top sirloin and call it chile Colorado. It may not be what you think of as chile Colorado. You can also do this recipe with leftover turkey from Thanksgiving. I recommend you do. It's stupid-good. Some grocers mistakenly list poblano peppers as pasilla peppers—make sure you get the dried peppers for this.

Season the beef with salt and pepper.

In a 10-inch cast-iron skillet over medium-high heat, warm the vegetable oil. Working in four batches, sear the beef until it is browned, about 2 minutes per batch. You don't want it cooked too much, just coated with oil and browned. Using a slotted spoon, transfer the beef to another container.

In the same pan, over medium heat, sauté the yellow onion and cumin seeds until the onion is translucent, about 3 minutes. Add the tomatoes, tomatillos, garlic, pasilla, dried chiles, and bay leaves and cook for 30 minutes, stirring occasionally, until the tomatillos are cooked and the chiles are soft. Turn the heat to medium-low and add the water to keep it saucy. Transfer to a blender and process to make the sauce as smooth as possible.

Return the meat to the pan and cover with the sauce. Serve family-style, with the tortillas and red onions, and let everybody make their own tacos.

3 pounds beef, preferably in one piece (hanger steak, hanging tender, or top sirloin), trimmed and cut into ½-by-2-inch pieces (like for fajitas) or the equivalent of leftover turkey, breast chopped into pieces, and dark meat shredded by hand

Kosher salt

Freshly ground black pepper

1 tablespoon vegetable oil

1 yellow onion, thinly sliced

1 teaspoon cumin seeds

8 Roma tomatoes, chopped

1 cup husked, rinsed, and halved tomatillos

6 garlic cloves, minced

1 dried pasilla pepper (see headnote), stemmed and seeded

2 dried guajillo chiles, stemmed and seeded

1 dried chile morita, stemmed and seeded

2 bay leaves

1 cup water

16 to 18 corn tortillas, warmed (see page 29)

2 red onions, very thinly sliced

SERVES 4

MEXICAN-STYLE GUACAMOLE

Real Mexican guacamole doesn't have tomatoes, onion, or cilantro. That's an American thing, the "bigger is better" mentality. Real Mexican guacamole is all about the avocado. Add a little acidity but don't change the color. Add a little heat to give character. And add some salt to bring out the flavor. Just mix it all up, and you have magic. If you add anything else it becomes *guac-a-mole-ay*. This is guacamole. A lot of different cuisines have that one recipe that is perfectly simple. Like pesto, which is just basil, garlic, pine nuts, olive oil, and cheese. Hummus is just garbanzo, sesame paste, lemon juice, and olive oil.

5 avocados, pitted and peeled

Juice of 2 limes

1 serrano chile, with seeds, minced

Kosher salt

Freshly ground black pepper

Tortilla chips for serving

———

In a large bowl, mash the avocados thoroughly with a fork, keeping the texture coarse. Add the lime juice and serrano as you mash. Season with salt and pepper. Serve immediately with chips.

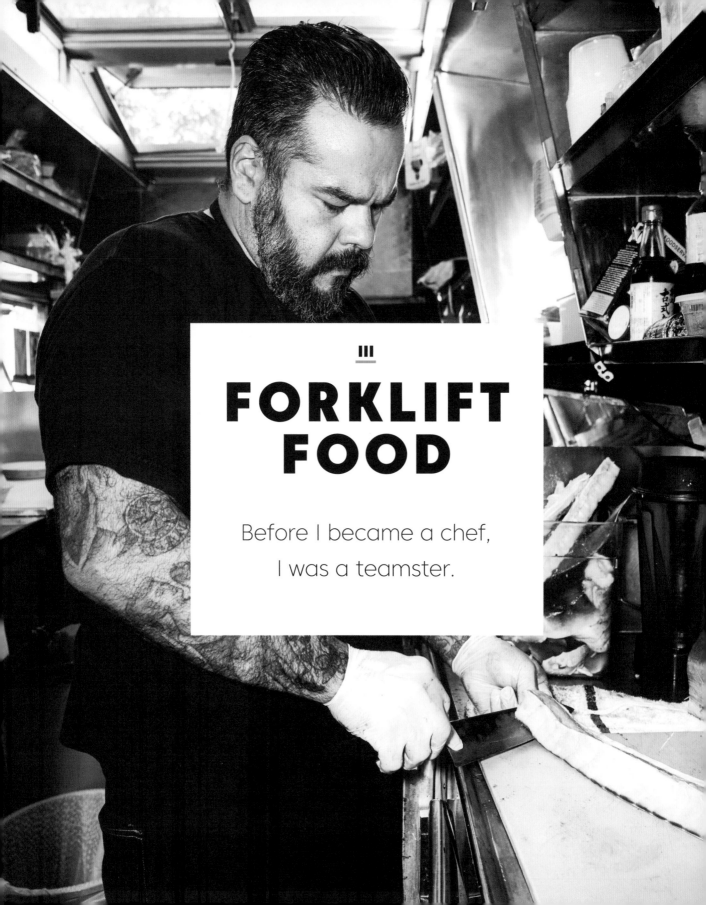

FORKLIFT FOOD

Before I became a chef,
I was a teamster.

A TEQUILA-FUELED FISHING TRIP TO MEXICO WITH THE TEAMSTERS LOCAL 848 WAS WHEN I REALIZED I COULD REALLY COOK.

After I moved out of the house in Pico, I got an apartment in Bellflower. For a while I tried out community college, while supporting myself working at a Pick 'N Save. But that did not last. Then my dad hooked me up at his workplace, Crockett Container, and I became a teamster, just like my dad, Jose Sr., a.k.a. "Chubbs," and my older brother, Jose Jr.

Crockett is a corrugated-fiberboard company in Sante Fe Springs, a small incorporated industrial area south of L.A., fairly close to Pico. Basically, they make cardboard boxes. Chubbs made the paper and cut it into the right shapes and sizes to be formed into the boxes, which was one of the cushy jobs at Crockett. I worked on the cascader, a big, metal, awful-loud machine that coats the paper in hot wax to create insulated cardboard for shipping vegetables. The cardboard became boxes, which would hold iced vegetables and keep them fresh for shipping. It was the worst job at the factory.

After treating the boxes, I'd stack them flat onto pallets and tie them down. Then I'd stack those pallets high—sometimes thousands of pounds of paper materials in a single stack. When I got promoted, I drove a forklift moving the stacks from place to place. It was loud, awful, back-breaking work.

But in a way, Crockett Container was my first job in food. After going through the cascader, the materials would be made into boxes, which were then shipped to farms all over California, to be loaded up with produce for transport. Napa cabbage, carrots, corn, bok choy, baby bok choy, Gailan bok choy—I first saw these words printed on the side of boxes at Crockett. Same with the names of farms—Happy Boy, Love Bunny, Muranaka. These are farms I now work with as a chef.

Being a teamster was alright. I had a uniform of the classic work shirt with my name on it. It offered good money, a good union, retirement, benefits, all that. Crockett was my dad's second job in America after emigrating from Mexico. He happened to work at a car wash around the corner from where the factory opened and got in on the ground floor. For him, being a teamster was what enabled him to provide for his kids, even after Mom died. It's the kind of job you stay in for life—you join up when you're young, you get married, you have kids. You watch your kids in little league, you drink beer after work, you get fat. You retire. You die.

I knew it wasn't for me forever. I wasn't being challenged at Crockett. I was just another cog in the wheel. And I wasn't following a passion.

But at the same time, I was in my early twenties and I was making good money for the first time. I got a decent apartment. After a while, I got a nice car, and around the time I got the car, I remember I started smoking weed.

I had never had any interest in weed before that. I was super straight-laced until my mom died, and then I remember looking through her stuff after she passed and finding some pot, I guess for the pain she was in toward the end. I vowed never to try it.

My roommate from my first apartment and I were really into *Mr. Show*, a skit comedy show with David Cross and Bob Odenkirk that was just hilarious. We'd record the episodes on VHS when they aired and watch them over and over again at night. One day we were watching *Mr. Show* and my roommate pulled out a joint. I remember thinking, okay, why not? I smoked it and then BAM—the whole room changed and I was just laughing at *Mr. Show* in a way I never had, and I remember very clearly thinking to myself, "Why on Earth have I not smoked weed before?"

After that it was all over for the next couple years. I was a wake-and-bake stoner. I'd go straight from the forklift, maybe stopping for dinner somewhere, to the apartment, where I'd smoke weed with my roommate and watch TV or listen to the Beatles. Go to bed, wake and bake, and get back to the forklift. Forklift, home, weed, Beatles, bed, forklift. Repeat.

On the weekends we'd go out drinking and get torn up, just getting around a little and experiencing L.A. nightlife for real. Sometimes we'd catch a late-night movie like *Requiem for a Dream* at the Sunset Five. One night we dropped acid at a nightclub in Hollywood and went dancing with all these mod girls wearing go-go boots. It was fun.

Notice I have not mentioned eating or cooking. At that point, I didn't even know how to cook beans. I was pretty busy with work and just decompressing during my downtime. I remember eating out at a lot of restaurants I hadn't been to as a kid, places I thought at the time were "fancy," but not ones I'd eat at today. But I didn't know. Restaurants like Olive Garden, Soup Plantation, Yard House. The best place I'd probably eaten was Twin Palms in Pasadena. They're alright, and at the time, I thought they were nice because I didn't know about food. (My nephew who works for me is nineteen and he's already going to Providence, which is probably the best restaurant in all of Los Angeles. He's on the right track. But I didn't have those kinds of influences at the time.)

Probably the best food I'd had was the stuff cooked by my mom at home, or my grandmother, Chubbs' mother, in Mexico. Chubbs is from a tiny town in Durango called Mendoza. Super-country. He grew up in an adobe house. The food comes from what's around—beans and corn they grow themselves, maybe a local pig killed that week. That's where I ate the best as a kid. And I ate well in Baja, where I had my first shellfish. But when I was working at Crockett, I didn't know where to find stuff like that, nor could I duplicate it myself at home. All my money went to eating out, but it wasn't at the right places. Food was always a top priority, just not always something I could create myself.

Eventually I started whipping up stuff at home just to see if I could. And I found that, actually, I could cook beans. I started easy. A lot of bacon, a lot of potatoes. Hot dogs with eggs. Just fat and protein. And because I was such a fat-ass kid and obsessed with food I soon realized could actually remember a lot of what my mom used to cook and how to do it.

One night I tried to make my mom's albondigas. It took me three hours, but it turned out okay. I had a knack for tasting and adjusting, for figuring out in my head how to make things taste the way I want them to. And I kept trying it. I got good at it. Before long, I was making my mom's albondigas—almost as good as she used to make—in just forty minutes. That was definitely a breakthrough.

So cooking was becoming a hobby for me, but I was still a little shifty and just young. I had started selling weed on the side, not so much for the money but basically because I didn't like having to hang out for hours smoking bowls and playing video games at my weed dealer's house just to get some pot. (Do kids still do that? Why does the weed dealer always hold you hostage with the videos games?)

Once I started, even though it wasn't my livelihood, I found I was good at selling weed. And later I'd come to see that selling weed is just like selling tacos—it's about mark-ups, margins, and moving product. It's about keeping your customer happy. It's about providing variety and also dependability.

So there were some stoner food experiments in those years like Taco Pasta: Lawry's seasoning with ground beef, spaghetti, and Monterey Jack cheese instead of parm. I washed it down with a cold lager. For some reason I thought that Taco Pasta was the shit. I still think it kind of is, but I get why it's a little weird for people. But before passing judgment, try the recipe (see page 81). Is that or is that not delicious? You don't have to be stoned, but it can't hurt.

I guess I was taking baby steps, developing recipes on my own for the first time, but it was all just for me, not yet for other people.

All the shipping and receiving guys at Crockett take a big fishing trip once a year. Usually around August or September, there's a weekend down in Ensenada. Everybody goes. Dozens of guys from ages twenty-two to sixty-five. We drove down in a caravan across the border. It was a Friday and that night we had a huge rager in town. Just buckets of beer and tequila were consumed. I was so messed up. Then the next day fishing, we were still drinking tequila from the bottle on the boat. I'd never been fishing before. And I was drunk as shit. I think there's a photo of me on the boat. I think I have frosted tips and I'm holding a beer. Suffice it to say, I was not in much of a state to catch my first fish.

But there isn't that much to it—just put the sardine on the hook, throw in the line, and see what bites. My first time out, I caught six albacore, two yellow tail, and one bigeye. The biggest fish I caught was 65 pounds. I mean, I crushed it. Beginners luck, I guess. We filleted them and threw them in an ice chest and drove them back to L.A. on Sunday night after stopping in Puerto Nuevo for lobster. Between all the teamsters, we caught one hundred thirty-seven albacore on that trip.

So on Sunday I got back to my Norwalk apartment and I had all this fish. And I didn't know what to do with it. So I called up my dad. And he told me how to make ceviche out of it. A bunch of lime, a bunch of sliced chile, some spices, and oil. I made some that night. And it tasted fucking awesome.

I called up some friends. "Yo, you have to come over, I have all this food." My buddy brought a keg of Dos Equis. We had the ceviche and used my Weber to grill the rest of the fish I caught. A whole bunch of people came over that night and we all ate and drank like kings. I made late-night taco pasta. Everybody loved it.

That was a profound experience for me. Not only was I cooking tasty food for my friends for the first time, not only did they like it, but this was also the first fish I had caught and killed myself. You have to stick those albacore with a pole to kill them. It might sound cheesy but that does give you respect for the food, for where it came from and the fact that it died for you. It was like a rite of passage for me, something I'll never forget. It's part of becoming a cook.

Since the teamsters go down to Ensenada every year, I figured this was the beginning of a great tradition, of albacore cookouts and mounds of ceviche and friends and kegs of beer at the apartment. Of course, even though I went on the fishing trip every year I worked at Crockett, I never caught dick again. But after that first trip and the party at the apartment in Norwalk, I knew for sure I could do this.

I knew I could cook.

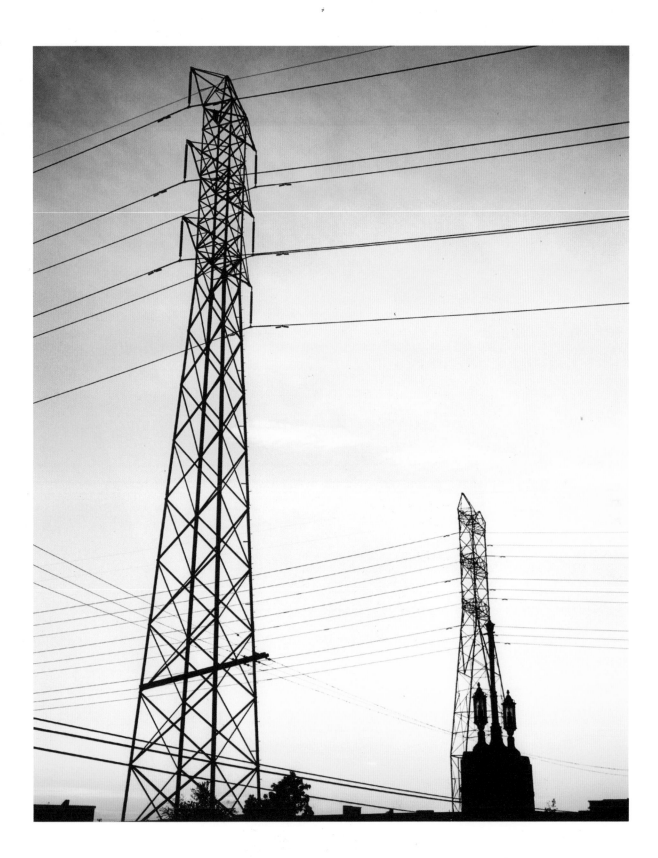

SUNCHOKE TACO

One week, baby artichokes were not available but sunchokes were; so they went on the menu. Sunchokes are also known as "Jerusalem artichokes" because their flavor is similar to an artichoke. Here, we cook the sunchokes in milk and then sauté in butter. Cooking in milk helps keep the sunchokes white, and the colors of the pomegranate and Brussels sprouts make for a beautiful taco.

In a 4-quart saucepan over medium-high heat, combine the sunchokes and milk. Bring to a simmer, add the salt, and then turn the heat to medium-low. After 12 minutes, pierce a sunchoke with a knife; it should feel as soft as a boiled potato. Remove from the heat and reserve.

To make the pomegranate salsa: In a 10-inch cast-iron skillet over medium-high heat, warm 1 tablespoon of the olive oil. Add the onion and thyme, season with salt and pepper, and sauté until nicely browned, about 3 minutes. Using a spatula, carefully turn the discs onto their other sides and brown another 3 minutes; we're looking for a charred texture, not a sautéed onion texture. Transfer the onion to a cutting board and, with a sharp knife, dice into ¼-inch pieces. Place the onion in a large bowl and add the pomegranate seeds, serrano, chives, parsley, macadamias, vinegar, and remaining 3 tablespoons olive oil and stir to mix. Set aside.

Peel the Brussels sprouts leaves from each other, using your fingers and working from the roots to the tips. Maintain their shape as much as possible. Line a plate with paper towels.

In a 6-inch cast-iron skillet over medium-high heat, warm the vegetable oil to 350°F. Add the sprout leaves in batches, a layer at a time, and fry until golden brown. Using a slotted spoon, transfer to the prepared plate and season with salt. Set aside. Discard the oil.

In the same skillet, over medium-high heat, melt the butter. Drain the sunchokes and add them to the skillet along with the thyme. Sauté until golden brown, about 5 minutes.

Layer the sunchokes and Brussels sprout leaves on each tortilla, then top with the salsa. Serve immediately.

1 pound sunchokes, peeled and cut into bite-size pieces

4 cups whole milk

1 tablespoon kosher salt

Pomegranate Salsa

4 tablespoons extra-virgin olive oil

1 medium red onion, sliced into ½-inch discs (try to keep the discs intact, so they are closed circles)

2 thyme sprigs

Kosher salt

Freshly ground black pepper

Seeds of 1 large pomegranate

1 serrano chile, with seeds, stemmed and finely minced

⅛ cup minced chives

⅛ cup minced parsley

¼ cup chopped roasted macadamia nuts

2 tablespoons sherry vinegar

6 large Brussels sprouts, stemmed

1 cup vegetable oil

Kosher salt

2 tablespoons unsalted butter

1 thyme sprig

6 corn tortillas, warmed (see page 29)

BRISKET TACO

I first started cooking brisket after a trip to Tradewinds Ranch on Oahu. We were trying to source local foods to cook with and to pair with the local produce we had available at the ranch. We found this and cooked it in fat the next day for breakfast. When you cook brisket, it can get dry, which is why I confit it in beef lard. The end product is rich and unctuous and it's a really nice way to present this cut of meat. We pair it with sumac onions and herbs, and an arbol salsa. It takes me right back to that trip to Oahu.

2 quarts beef or pork lard

One 4-pound brisket, cut into large cubes about 1 by 2 inches

Kosher salt

Freshly ground black pepper

Sumac Onions

2 red onions, julienned

⅛ cup sumac

¼ cup washed and torn mint leaves

Leaves torn from 2 oregano sprigs

20 corn tortillas, warmed (see page 29)

Arbol Salsa (page 34) for topping

1 cup micro chives

Preheat the oven to 275°F.

In a large Dutch oven over medium-high heat, melt the lard. Season the brisket with salt and pepper and then add to the Dutch oven; it should be submerged. Once the lard comes to a simmer, turn the heat to low. Cover with the lid and place in the oven. Cook slow and low for 8 hours.

To make the sumac onions: About 30 minutes before serving, in a large mixing bowl, combine the onions, sumac, mint leaves, and oregano and toss to mix. Set aside.

Remove the Dutch oven from the oven and set on the stove top.

Using a slotted spoon, evenly portion out the brisket to the tortillas. Add some sumac onions to each, top with a dollop of salsa, and garnish with the micro chives. Serve immediately. You're eating well tonight.

SWORDFISH TACO

This is my version of California cuisine—very much a farm-to-table meal. You're using red frill mustard greens and tangerines, which tend to be available in the spring here. It's just a Mediterranean-style seafood dish with nice ingredients.

About 1 hour before you're ready to eat, remove the fish from the refrigerator and season with the salt. Let come to room temperature.

In a 12-inch cast-iron skillet over medium-high heat, warm the butter. Add the swordfish and cook until 90 percent medium done, about 4 minutes. It should firm up slightly and look golden brown in places. Flip the pieces and cook on the other side for 12 seconds. Remove with a slotted spatula to a plate and set aside.

In a large mixing bowl, immediately and quickly mix the mustard greens with the olive oil and vinegar—toss to just coat.

Portion the swordfish pieces onto each tortilla, then add the tangerines and mustard greens. Garnish with as much salsa as you like and squeeze the limes over the top. Serve immediately.

2 pounds swordfish fillet, cut into 2-ounce pieces

1 tablespoon kosher salt

2 tablespoons unsalted butter

12 sprigs of red frill mustard greens, or other spicy greens, washed and torn into bite-size pieces

2 tablespoons olive oil

1 tablespoon sherry vinegar

12 corn tortillas, warmed (see page 29)

4 seedless tangerines, peeled and sectioned

Salsa del Valle (page 133) for garnishing

3 limes, cut into quarters

SERVES 4 (3 TAQUITOS EACH)

FRIED POTATO TAQUITO

I can eat, like, six of these. You can make these and leave them in the fridge and eat them the next day. Just like a party snack—my version of the Cielito Lindo fried beef taquito. Probably my oldest memory of eating taquitos in my life is from Cielito Lindo. It's an L.A. institution, on the corner of Cesar Chavez and Alameda at the entrance to Olvera Street. I love that place. They still make my favorite taquito. If somebody asked me what my favorite taco in L.A. is, I'd say that.

Avocado-Tomatillo Salsa

1 pound tomatillos (preferably tomatillos milperos, the small purple-colored ones about the size of a quarter), husked and rinsed

2 avocados, pitted and peeled

4 serrano chiles, stemmed

6 garlic cloves, peeled

1 bunch of cilantro (reserve a few sprigs for garnishing the tacos), ends torn off (grab the bunch about 3 inches above the end of the stem and twist like you're ringing a towel, and discard the ends)

Kosher salt

4 to 6 limes

4 pounds any starchy potato, such as Yukon golds or russets

1½ pounds unsalted butter, at room temperature

Kosher salt

Freshly ground black pepper

12 large (6-inch) corn tortillas, warmed (see page 29)

¼ cup lard

Sea salt

2 cups rough-cut or grated aged cheddar cheese

To make the avocado-tomatillo salsa: In a food processor, combine the tomatillos, avocados, serranos, garlic, and cilantro and season with salt. Juice the limes on top. Cover the processor and hit it three or four times—pop, pop, pop—then let it blend a while. You'll start to see the seeds but keep it chunky. Taste it and season with more salt. Set aside.

Bring a big pot of salty water to a simmer. Throw in the potatoes and cook them thoroughly, about 17 minutes. Actually, you kind of want to overcook them. When they're super-soft, drain the potatoes in a colander. When the potatoes are cool, use a paring knife to peel them. Place the peeled potatoes in a big bowl and mash them roughly—you want to keep some of that texture and chunkiness. Add the butter and season with kosher salt and pepper.

Add 3 tablespoons potatoes to each of the tortillas and roll them into taquitos about 1½ inches in diameter.

In a 12-inch cast-iron skillet over medium-high heat, melt the lard. Add the taquitos and cook until golden brown, 4 to 6 minutes. Place the taquitos on a wire rack to cool and immediately season with sea salt. When the taquitos are cool enough to eat, garnish them with a good portion of salsa and cheddar on top. Serve immediately.

CARNITAS

I don't make carnitas like my mom. I make it like Thomas Keller's duck confit with green salt. Green salt isn't necessarily for seasoning; it's more just to extract liquid so when meat cooks it cooks completely in fat and gets really tender and soft. Carnitas is really confitted pork. But if you get it at any place on the street it might be boiled pork crisped up with fat on the plancha. But that's not really good. The salting process here is not Mexican at all. I use a whole bone-in, skin-on pork shoulder. The key is to *not* make a small batch.

The salsa casera is a simple tomato-based chile. It's the easiest, most versatile salsa I make. You can use it as a base, crack eggs in it to make a Mexican shakshuka, dress it up with cilantro—anything you want. It goes great with carnitas.

My co-author Richard, a.k.a. RP3, came up with this jalapeño-onion-carrot escabeche recipe. It's a great addition to sandwiches, eggs, and probably as a riff accompaniment to literally any other recipe in this book. (Store in an airtight container in the fridge for up to 2 weeks.)

You can start this recipe in the morning and have your dinner party at night. Or, start it at night and sleep while the pork cooks in your oven and have it ready for the next day.

To make the green salt: In a food processor or blender, combine the bay leaves, thyme leaves, parsley, sugar, salt, oregano, and serranos and pulse until it has the consistency of wet sand.

Rub the green salt over the pork, completely coating it. Put the pork on a metal rack in a roasting pan (to catch the drippings), and place in the fridge for at least 4 hours but no longer than 12 hours.

Preheat the oven to 325°F.

Remove the pork from the fridge and rinse off the salt. Pat dry. The pork should have a light green color. Wrap the pork tightly in oven-safe plastic wrap and then twice in aluminum foil. Place in a roasting pan deep enough to catch any fat that renders off. Roast for 7 hours.

continued

Green Salt

4 bay leaves, preferably fresh (if not available, use the same amount of dried)

2 tablespoons fresh thyme leaves

¼ cup dried parsley

1 tablespoon sugar

6 tablespoons kosher salt

1 tablespoon oregano, preferably fresh (if not available, use the same amount of dried)

2 serrano chiles, stemmed

One 4- to 6-pound piece pork, preferably a bone-in, skin-on shoulder piece

Salsa Casera

4 Roma tomatoes

2 serrano chiles, stemmed

4 garlic cloves, peeled

Kosher salt

Jalapeño-Onion-Carrot Escabeche

3 cups water

2 cups white vinegar

½ cup sugar, preferably cane sugar

1 tablespoon kosher salt

3 whole cloves

8 peppercorns

5 allspice berries

1 bay leaf

1 star anise

1 tablespoon mustard seeds

8 jalapeño chiles, with seeds, stemmed and sliced into ¼-inch coins

1 white onion, ends removed, halved vertically, and each half cut into 8 wedges, again, vertically

3 carrots, peeled and diagonally cut into ¼-inch coins

24 corn tortillas, warmed (see page 29)

To make the salsa casera: Bring a 4-quart pot of water to a boil over high heat. Add the tomatoes and cook until soft, about 6 minutes. Using a slotted spoon, transfer the tomatoes to a blender. Add the serranos and garlic, blend until smooth, and season with salt. (If you won't be eating immediately, transfer to an airtight container and refrigerate for up to 3 hours.)

To make the jalapeño-onion-carrot escabeche: In a large saucepan over high heat, combine the water, vinegar, sugar, salt, cloves, peppercorns, allspice berries, bay leaf, star anise, and mustard seeds. Bring the pickling liquid to a boil and boil for 5 minutes.

Meanwhile, put the jalapeños, onion, and carrots in a large ceramic bowl or baking dish. Pour the boiling-hot pickling liquid over the vegetables. Let steep for at least 1 hour or up to 3 hours. The liquid should slightly cook the vegetables and imbue them with delicious flavor.

Lower the oven temperature to 200°F. Remove the pork from the foil and plastic wrap. Carefully, find the bone and pull it out—it will slide right out of there. Transfer the meat to a cast-iron skillet and cover with foil. Place in the oven until you're ready to serve.

Place the pork, tortillas, escabeche, and salsa out on the table and let people tear it up. Use a fork or slotted spoon to serve the escabeche so diners can avoid eating the whole spices.

TACO PASTA

This is what Mexican moms give you when you ask for mac and cheese. Well, at least mine did. So did my aunts, and my friends' moms, too. It's just something you make from the pantry. Kids love it. Stoners love it. Cooks love it. I've made this for staff meal at some of L.A.'s finer restaurants, and it's always a big hit.

One time at Marché, I made taco pasta with leftover cavatelli with pig ears, pork belly, beef stock, fancy Normandy butter, and fresh herbs. It was so good. This is based on that recipe. The basic pieces are some kind of taco-like spice mixture (that's the "taco" part) and then some kind of starch (that's the "pasta" part) to get you through a long service.

In a 10-inch cast-iron skillet over medium-high heat, melt the lard. Add the rigatoni and cook until the pasta tubes turn golden brown, some a little darker, about 4 minutes. Using a slotted spoon, remove the pasta, leaving the lard in the pan. Lower the heat while removing the pasta to minimize the splatter. Set the pasta aside.

To the same pan, add the ground beef, bring the heat back to medium, and cook until the beef is brown, about 7 minutes. Using the slotted spoon, transfer the beef to a plate and set aside. Add the onion to the pan and sauté until translucent, about 3 minutes. Add the garlic, garlic powder, onion powder, cumin, red pepper flakes, parsley, and 2 teaspoons black pepper and cook until aromatic, about 30 seconds. Add the cooked ground beef and tomato sauce and simmer for 10 minutes. Remove from the heat.

Fill a large stockpot halfway with water. Add salt until it's as salty as the sea. Set over high heat and, once the water reaches a rolling boil, add the pasta and cook for 7 to 9 minutes, or until al dente.

Keeping the pasta in the pot, pour out all but 3 tablespoons of the water and return to the stove over medium-low heat. Immediately add the meat sauce to the stockpot along with all the cheese and cook until thoroughly mixed and the cheese is fully melted, about 1 minute. Taste the pasta and adjust the seasoning with salt and lots of cracked black pepper.

Serve immediately with the bread.

½ cup lard

1 pound rigatoni

1 pound ground beef

1 white onion, chopped

4 garlic cloves, peeled and sliced lengthwise

1 teaspoon garlic powder

1 teaspoon onion powder

1 teaspoon ground cumin

1 teaspoon dried red pepper flakes

1 tablespoon dried parsley

Cracked black pepper

One 16-ounce can tomato sauce or one 8-ounce can tomato paste mixed with 1 cup water

Kosher salt

4 ounces Monterey Jack cheese, cut into cubes

4 ounces cheddar cheese, cut into cubes

4 slices white bread

CRAB AND SPIGARELLO TOSTADA

I like using local stone crab from Santa Barbara because it's sweet and the meat has nice texture. You have to be careful cleaning them because the shells are brittle and will break off, which is probably why you don't see the crab around too much. To save yourself the trouble, you can substitute one 8-ounce can of premium crab meat.

Fill a small saucepan three-quarters full with water. Add salt until it's as salty as the sea. Set over high heat and, once the water reaches a rolling boil, throw in the spigarello. Cook for 15 seconds and then use a spider to transfer to paper towels to drain.

Prepare an ice-water bath in the largest mixing bowl you have by stirring together water and a tray of ice.

In an 8-quart stockpot filled three-quarters full with water,combine the carrots, celery, onion, peppercorns, lemon juice, bay leaves, parsley, and ¼ cup salt. Set over high heat and bring to a boil, about 2 minutes. Add the stone crab and cook for 8 minutes. Then, using a spider, transfer the crab to the ice-water bath and let cool for 10 minutes.

Using kitchen shears, cut off the legs. Use your thumb to remove the crab's body from the shell and then use a seafood fork to remove the meat from the body. Use the shears and seafood fork to remove the meat from the legs and claws. Set the meat aside.

Line a wire rack with paper towels.

In a 12-inch cast-iron skillet over medium-high heat, warm the vegetable oil to about 375°F. Add the tortillas and fry until crispy, about 30 seconds per side. Or, put the tortillas right over the flame of the range until they're blistering and dry. Season the tortillas with salt after pulling them from the oil or fire. Let the tostadas cool on the prepared rack, until they're slightly warm. (You can also buy tostada shells.)

Divide the crab meat among the tostadas, then top with the tomato, salsa, and spigarello and garnish with the dill. Serve immediately.

Kosher salt

6 spigarello sprigs, washed, cut in half horizontally, and blanched, you can substitute spinach or kale

1 cup peeled rough-chopped carrots

1 cup rough-chopped celery

1 cup rough-chopped yellow onion

6 peppercorns

Juice of 1 lemon

2 bay leaves

4 Italian parsley sprigs

1 stone crab, or 8 ounces crab meat

¼ cup vegetable oil

6 corn tortillas

1 large heirloom tomato, halved and sliced into bite-size pieces

Almond Salsa (page 30) for topping

1 fresh dill sprig, torn into 6 attractive pieces

RAZOR CLAMS À LA PLANCHA

Razor clams always remind me of my time spent in Tarragona in the Costa del Sol region in Spain. Tanya and I had them at this place called L'Ancora. They don't skimp there—it's so abundant, it's ridiculous!

Anjojoli Salsa

4 Roma tomatoes, halved

4 pickled cascabella peppers

3 guajillo chiles, stemmed and toasted in olive oil until aromatic

2 tablespoons sesame seeds

1 tablespoon pine nuts

¼ cinnamon stick

1 teaspoon ground cumin

½ cup white vinegar

¼ cup extra-virgin olive oil

1½ tablespoons sugar

Kosher salt

1 recipe Preserved Lemons (page 137)

1½ pounds razor clams (shells included)

3 tablespoons cornmeal

2 tablespoons extra-virgin olive oil

1 lemon, quartered

1 tablespoon finishing olive oil

¼ cup torn micro shiso leaves

1 tablespoon sesame seeds

To make the anjojoli salsa: In a 4-quart stockpot, combine the tomatoes and enough water to just cover. Bring to a boil over high heat, then lower the heat and simmer until the tomatoes are fork-tender, about 8 minutes. Drain off half the liquid and add the cascabellas, guajillos, sesame seeds, pine nuts, cinnamon, cumin, vinegar, olive oil, sugar, and 1 tablespoon salt. Simmer for 3 minutes and then transfer to a blender. Blend on high speed until totally smooth. Taste and season with additional salt, if desired. Set aside. (If reserving for longer than 3 hours, transfer to an airtight container and refrigerate for up to 1 day.)

In a nonstick pan over medium-low heat, layer the preserved lemons and let brown, about 1 minute per side. (They have sugar and salt on them so they should caramelize pretty quickly.) Set aside.

Place the razor clams in a pot standing with the shell openings up. (Razor clams are always slightly open.) Place the pot under the faucet and turn on the water to the lowest possible flow. Fill the pot with water and then keep the water running, overflowing into the sink. Sprinkle 1 tablespoon of the cornmeal into the pot about 1 minute later and keep the water running. The cornmeal helps the clams filter out the sand. After about 10 minutes, drain the water, rinse the pot, and repeat the process. Then repeat it again. You have to do it three times because razor clams are sandy. After three rinsings, the clams are ready to use.

continued

Place a large (12-inch or greater) skillet over medium-high heat and coat with the extra-virgin olive oil. Add as many clams as you can in a single layer; you want them flush with the pan. Depending on the size of your pan, you'll be working in batches; if you're using a 12-inch skillet, you'll be working in two batches. Cover the pan and steam the clams for 4 minutes, or until the clams open wider. Remove the clams from the skillet and place on a baking sheet. Repeat the process until all the clams are cooked.

Transfer four or five clams to each serving plate and squeeze the lemon over. Drizzle liberally with the salsa and finishing olive oil and then top with the shiso leaves and sesame seeds. Serve immediately.

SHRIMP AGUACHILE

When I was a kid we didn't have high-end ceviche with fresh shrimp, halibut, or ingredients like that. My dad loves ceviche but he used imitation *jaiba*—crab. Add a little lemon and chile to that. It's not bad. It wasn't until I was a teenager that I tasted real marinated fish ceviche. It's totally different, imitation crab ceviche can be just as good, but it is a different dish. And then I tried aguachile. That was my jam. Basically, it's chile water—whatever raw seafood you're using, totally submerged in liquid. A ceviche is like a salad. But this is a lot more liquid-y, and it's way spicier. I use real shrimp in my aguachile, but the spice mixture and preparation is just as simple as it was when my dad was making ceviche for us in the house in Pico.

In a bowl, mix together the habanero salsa and salsa bruja to make an aguachile. Set aside.

Using a paring knife, cut the shrimp from their tops to the bottoms of the tails. Make a small incision to the point where it's almost cut through and slowly move the knife down to the bottom, and open up each like a book.

Layer the shrimp in a shallow bowl and pour the aguachile over until the shrimp are covered. (If necessary, use more salsa bruja sauce to fully cover the shrimp.) Sprinkle a generous amount of salt over the top. Let marinate for 5 minutes; the shrimp should start changing color and also cook in the acid.

Add the gooseberries, onion, and cilantro to the shrimp. Garnish generously with the olive oil. You want to taste the fattiness of the olive oil with all that acidity. Serve immediately on the tostadas.

1 recipe Roasted Habanero-Serrano Salsa (page 47)

1 recipe Salsa Bruja (page 45)

2 pounds (16/20 size) shrimp (see headnote, page 176), shelled and deveined

Maldon salt

1 cup cape gooseberries, husked and washed, or cherry tomatoes, halved

1 large red onion, very thinly sliced

1 cup rough-chopped cilantro

2 tablespoons extra-virgin olive oil

8 tostada shells

ALBONDIGAS

This is the soup that made my wife fall in love with me. My mom made it when I was a kid. It's a meal that's made to share—you shouldn't make just a little *albondigas* (meatballs). Make a huge batch for a dinner party, or just give it to your friends and neighbors. They'll fall in love with you, too.

Oh, and by the way, keep your eye on this soup when you're making it. When my mom would make this soup, I couldn't resist grazing and just eating the albondigas when nobody was looking. Pick one out, munch it, pick one out, munch it—soon you're out of meatballs.

Meatballs

4 pounds lean (90%) ground beef

2 pounds ground pork

1 cup uncooked long grain rice

1 cup chopped fresh mint

1½ tablespoons kosher salt

2 teaspoons cracked black pepper

4 garlic cloves, peeled and minced

2 tablespoons vegetable oil, olive oil, or lard

2 cups diced yellow onions

6 carrots, peeled and cut diagonally into 3-inch pieces

3 stalks celery, peeled, tough threads removed, and cut diagonally into 3-inch pieces

3 cups chopped red-skinned potatoes (1-by-2-inch chunks)

3 tablespoons tomato paste

12 ounces canned tomato sauce

To make the meatballs: In a large bowl, combine the beef, pork, rice, mint, salt, pepper, and garlic and mix well with your hands. Once the ingredients are fully incorporated, form into balls about 2 ounces each, about the size of a golf ball, and set aside on a plate.

In an 8-quart stockpot over medium-low heat, combine the vegetable oil, onions, carrots, celery, and potatoes. Turn the heat to high and cook until the onions are translucent, about 5 minutes. Add the tomato paste, tomato sauce, bay leaf, cumin, and chicken stock and let come to a simmer.

Once the stock is steaming, start adding the meatballs, one by one, until they're all in there. Tuck them under the surface if any are sticking out—they should fit perfectly. The meatballs will cool the stock down, so adjust the heat as you go to keep it at a low simmer. The stock should be red. Allow the meatballs to simmer for about 45 minutes. Do *not* stir for the first 10 to 20 minutes, or until the meatballs are cooked through—otherwise you risk breaking them apart, which you don't want. Skim any scum from the surface as you go.

continued

After 45 minutes, remove a meatball and cut into it. You'll know they're done when the rice is cooked. When the meatballs are done, season with salt and turn off the heat. The soup will stay hot for a while.

Serve the soup, ballparking four or five meatballs per portion, and garnish with the limes, cheese, avocados, chiles, and cilantro to your liking. (You might have leftovers, and you'll be glad if you do. Store in an airtight container in the fridge for up to 2 days.)

1 bay leaf

1 teaspoon ground cumin

4 quarts chicken stock, or broth made from bouillon

Kosher salt

6 limes, halved

16 ounces panela cheese or queso fresco, cut into 3-inch strips

2 avocados, pitted, quartered, peeled, and sliced very thin

2 serranos chiles, with seeds, sliced very thin

1 habanero chile, sliced very thin

Leaves torn from 5 cilantro sprigs

POZOLE

When it comes to cooking a whole pig, pozole is the end of the line. Tripe and the offcuts go into Menudo (page 96). Organ meats get stewed and turned into blood sausage. But all the other stuff, the super-weird, super-offcuts, go into pozole. That means head, ears, bones, whatever.

My dad makes a good pozole. The trick is using those crazy offcuts. You know your pozole is ready to eat when the pig ear is tender and you can bite right through it. The ears take the longest to get tender; it goes from being the texture of a piece of leather to that of a gummy bear.

We make this for Christmas at my dad's house. You have to skim like crazy the whole time it's cooking because all that funk and all those impurities will rise to the surface. When you put the leftovers in the fridge, after a few hours, you should be able to cut through the soup like pâté.

This is a crazy-delicious soup that you'd make after slaughtering a pig and after you've used everything good from that pig. There is going to be a pig's foot in this soup. This is a gnarly soup! Do not make it if you are the timid type. You're gonna need a big—32-quart—stockpot and some calcium hydroxide, a.k.a. pickling lime, edible lime, hydrated lime, or slaked lime (if you are unable to source locally, you can order this online). If you don't want to cook the dried hominy yourself, you can substitute 8 cups prepared hominy.

1 cup calcium hydroxide

5 cups dried Anson Mills pencil cob hominy

2 tablespoons lard

8 guajillo chiles, stemmed and seeded

2 dried pasilla chiles, stemmed and seeded

4 dried red New Mexican chiles, stemmed and seeded

4 chiles cascabel, stemmed and seeded

8 black peppercorns

In a large (10- or 16-quart) stainless-steel pot over high heat, bring 8 quarts water to a simmer. Add the calcium hydroxide and stir with a spoon until it is dissolved. Add the dried hominy and cook for 2 minutes. Remove the pot from the heat, cover with the lid, and let stand on the stove top overnight.

The next day, there will be a thin cloudy layer on top of the water. Pour that off. Using a mesh strainer, drain the water and transfer the hominy into another large pot. Fill that pot with fresh water and, as it's filling, agitate with your hands to remove the skins from the hominy kernels and any excess calicum. When the water gets cloudy, pour off the water. Repeat this process three times, or until all the calcium and skins are removed.

In the same pot, cover the hominy with cold, clean water. Bring it just to a simmer—a very, very low simmer, just slightly bubbling—and cook, uncovered, for 5 hours. Stir occasionally and add more water if the water level starts dropping below the kernels. After 5 hours, pull out a few kernels and rinse. Taste the hominy, it should still have a slight bite but be completely cooked. Drain off the hot liquid and give the hominy one more rinse in cold water. Set aside.

In a medium saucepan over medium heat, melt the lard. Add all the chiles, the peppercorns, cloves, and 1 tablespoon salt and toast until aromatic, about 5 minutes. Add the tomatoes, onions, bay leaves, and garlic and cook until the vegetables are softened and breaking apart under the weight of a wooden spoon, about 20 minutes. It will be thick but you want it thick. Once the tomatoes are soft, transfer to a blender and blend until very smooth—blend the shit out of it. Return the blended mixture to the saucepan. Add the vinegar and cook over medium heat for 2 minutes, stirring. Season with more salt. Set aside.

Add the ½ pig head, pig's feet, and spareribs to a 32-quart stockpot, cover with cold water, and place over high heat. Once the water boils, turn off the heat. You should see some impurities floating in the water. Drain the water and run cold water over the meats, rubbing your hands over the head and feet to dislodge any impurities.

Set the meats aside and clean the pot—it's going to be gunky so you have to wash it. Then, return the meats to that same pot along with the pork shoulder and pig ears. Cover with cold water and bring up the heat until the water is simmering. Simmer for 4 hours, adding water as needed in order to keep all the meat covered.

Once the meat is tender, stir in the chile-tomato mixture. Add the hominy, and season with salt.

Serve the soup garnished with a lot of shredded cabbage, sliced radishes, and as much salsa as you like. Do not pick out the bones. Go to town on a pig hoof!

3 whole cloves

Kosher salt

12 Roma tomatoes, halved

4 white onions, rough cut

4 bay leaves

8 garlic cloves, peeled

1 cup white vinegar, or as needed

½ pig head (about 5 pounds), ear reserved

4 pig's feet

1 rack of pork spareribs (about 2 pounds)

5 pounds bone-in pork shoulder, cut into 2- to 3-inch chunks (leave about 1 inch of meat around the bone piece)

7 pig ears (including the one from the ½ head), cut into 1-inch pieces

Shredded cabbage and sliced radishes for garnishing

Roasted Habanero-Serrano Salsa (page 47) for garnishing

MENUDO

This is a humble, country soup. You'll find similar peasant soups in the south of Spain, but here it's mixed with the spices and chiles of Mexico. There are four kinds of tripe: honeycomb tripe, book tripe (also known as bible tripe), cuajo tripe (also known as reed tripe), and plate tripe, my favorite. For me, plate tripe has the right texture and comes in long, wavy pieces.

My grandfather loves a cow's foot. Traditionally when you order menudo you'd say *"Dame lo con pata"* ("Give it to me with foot"). This is the way my grandfather always ordered it. It's fun to say. You don't get to say that very often.

2 tablespoons lard

8 guajillo chiles, stemmed and seeded

2 dried pasilla chiles, stemmed and seeded

4 dried red New Mexican chiles, stemmed and seeded

4 chiles cascabel, stemmed and seeded

3 whole cloves

Kosher salt

12 Roma tomatoes, halved

2 white onions, diced small, plus 3 cups diced white onions

8 garlic cloves, peeled

4 bay leaves

1 cup white vinegar, or as needed

6 pounds of beef tripe, cut into 2-by-2-inch pieces

2 cow trotters

4 pork trotters

3 cups chopped fresh cilantro, stems and leaves

1 cup dried oregano

1 cup dried red pepper flakes

Lots of lime, 1 or 2 per person, cut into wedges

In a medium saucepan over medium heat, melt the lard. Add all the chiles, the cloves, and 1 tablespoon salt and toast until aromatic, about 5 minutes. Add the tomatoes, small-diced onions, garlic, and bay leaves and cook until the vegetables are softened and breaking apart under the weight of a wooden spoon, about 20 minutes. It will be thick but you want it thick. Once the tomatoes are soft, transfer to a blender and blend until very smooth—blend the shit out of it. Return the blended mixture to the saucepan. Add the vinegar and cook over medium heat for 2 minutes, stirring. Set aside.

Add the tripe and trotters to a 32-quart stockpot, cover with cold water, and place over high heat. Once the water boils, turn off the heat. You should see some impurities floating in the water. Drain the water and run cold water over the meat, rubbing your hands over it to dislodge any impurities. Remove and discard the bones and rinse the meat under cold water.

Set the meat aside and clean the pot—it's going to be gunky so you have to wash it. Then, return the meat to that same pot. Cover with cold water and bring up the heat until the water is simmering. Simmer for 6 hours, adding water as needed in order to keep all the meat covered.

Once the meat is tender, add the chile-tomato mixture and season with salt.

Serve in big bowls. Allow diners to add as much of the diced onions, cilantro, oregano, red pepper flakes, and lime as they like.

IV

A CHEF'S JOURNEY

From culinary school to fine dining, and trying to find my way in the kitchen.

HINGS HAPPENED VERY QUICKLY FOR ME AND MY WIFE, TANYA.

Tanya was at that party at the apartment in Norwalk after the fishing trip. We had met at a nightclub in East Hollywood; this place called Miss Kitty's Parlour. Within the first couple times of hanging out with her, I was, like, I could picture marrying this girl.

en I met her, Tanya was miserable in her professional life, just like I was. She s commuting to UC Riverside, working on her doctorate in political science. But e didn't like political science. She wanted to do something more practical, less ademia. I asked her one day, "Why do you want to do this?" She said, "To be a fessor." I responded, "Why? So you can teach all the stuff you hate?" She had no swer, and she quit within a couple weeks. She switched tracks, pursuing a masters d then a doctorate in psychology. Now she's Dr. Mueller. She just did it—made a ge life decision like that with no fear. That was inspiring to watch.

nya saw how miserable I was working as a teamster. She motivated me to make ilar changes. She could tell I had greater ambitions. One night we were sitting und the apartment and I was feeling sorry for myself and she was, like, "Why don't u just quit? You like to cook right? Then cook!" I told her that yes I liked to cook home, but I didn't know anybody who was cooking professionally or was working in od restaurants. The world of fine restaurants and skilled cooking—to say nothing becoming a chef and owning a restaurant—felt very much out of my reach.

e next day, she booked me a tour at the California School of Culinary Arts in sadena, a division of Le Cordon Bleu.

e moment I walked in, I liked the feel of the place. Everybody was wearing white, erybody had something to do, there were a million little tasks being executed fectly at any given moment. And the smell. Culinary school always smelled like ck. Like a clean beef stock of roasted bones, celery, carrots, and onions simmering the stove. When a kitchen is clean, it should smell like that, because you should ays have a good stock going if you're going through restaurant-size portions animals and produce, and since it's all clean and orderly, you shouldn't smell ything else.

erms of sight, sound, smell, and overall vibe, it was the polar opposite of the ber factory I was working in. When I went to work the next day, I couldn't get that of my head. So I put in an application for culinary school. I had to go back to ool at night to get my GED because I actually never had finished high school.

I just didn't have enough credits when graduation came along, but they let me walk with the understanding that I'd finish the credits that summer. Of course, I didn't. So I was working at Crockett all day and taking classes at night for a couple months. That was crazy. It sounds kind of incredible to me now, but that's how badly I wanted out of that situation. That's how much I knew I was meant to be something and somebody else.

My dad was shocked when I told him. But he got it. He was actually stoked for me. He, like Tanya, knew I was not content to stay in my current situation. And my brother Jose, who also still worked at Crockett, just couldn't believe it. I think it blew his mind a little. And then a few months later, Jose followed my lead and quit himself. Nobody should stay in a job they don't like.

I started at the California School of Culinary Arts in Pasadena in February of 2004.

I loved culinary school. I thrived in it. I enjoyed the discipline. I discovered that I loved doing dishes, keeping everything neat and tidy. I loved starching my chef's hat and shirt, sharpening my knives, and I loved the satisfaction of getting really good at finely dicing a vegetable. Just a simple task like that had a built-in feeling of accomplishment for me. It's meditative work.

For the first time since my mother passed away, I was a good student again. I was never late. I did all my work perfectly without complaint. I was just obsessed with the work and progressing as a cook and didn't want to miss a thing. The one time I was tardy was when my car broke down and I had to take two buses from Diamond Bar, so I missed a few minutes of Baking 1.

At that point I was cooking at home for real. I miss those days because when you're a chef running a food truck, you have no time to cook at home. Now when I cook at home it's rice with a fried egg on it, with a little Sriracha. *If* I cook at home. But back then I was doing great, ambitious stuff at our apartment. Like, I would make crab eggs Benedict for breakfast. I'd make beignets. I'd make mole from scratch, which takes about two hours. I did my assigned work and more. I learned so many techniques. This would end up being a testing period for the first couple years of Guerrilla Tacos, when I did all of the prep, braising, salsas, marinating, etc., all in our home kitchen.

When I was in culinary school, Tanya was in school herself until 10 p.m. most nights. I'd usually be in the kitchen when she came back, making canapés, pâtés, or pastries, braising something, roasting something. . . . I loved the delicate side of cooking that

I discovered in culinary school, and the more scientific stuff, like baking. And I loved cooking for Tanya and our friends. There is no greater feeling than bringing joy by sharing food with others. It's the reason I do what I do, whether I'm cooking for friends or for total strangers.

Like I said, I loved culinary school. But knowing what I know now, I wouldn't do it again. And I wouldn't recommend that an aspiring chef go to culinary school. Because I ended up with $140,000 in student loan debt. They sell it well—they tell you you'll be making $60,000 a year when you get out. But you won't. Out of my class of eighty-something people, there are probably fewer than ten who are cooking professionally today.

But there was never any question for me once I made that life change. Once I graduated from culinary school, it was time to become an actual cook.

After school I got my first real job cooking at a restaurant called Viva Madrid in Claremont, California. It was a Spanish-style tapas place. The first thing they had me do was mince an entire case of parsley. That's a lot of parsley, like two dozen bunches. Chop, chop, chop. Then the chef used only a very little bit, in just two dishes. And he had made me mince it so thin we could have easily used a food processor. I was, like, why'd you have me do that? He was, like, just to see if you could do it. It sticks in my memory because that's a big part of surviving in a kitchen—when you're asked to do something, you can't spend too much time worrying about why. The reason why is that you've been told to do it by your chef. It can feel pointless but in the end all the experience serves to get you farther.

I could order anything I liked for lunch at Viva Madrid. So I ordered the oxtail stew. That was my first oxtail. I was, like, oh my God, where have you been all my life? So I started eating that for lunch every day at work.

I didn't feel very needed at Viva Madrid. The owner had two standard poodles who were basically her children that'd stay in the restaurant. My main job was cooking food for the dogs. I'd make steaks or chicken and grind it up and feed it to the dogs. I worked at Viva Madrid for three months before I was laid off. I guess I was eating too much oxtail and shrimp.

From there I started working as a baker at Whittier College. That was cushy. Cheesecakes, brownies, cookies, meringues, custards. I made it all from scratch. These students ate well while I was there. Baking is like making a mole—one or two off-flavors will throw the whole balance. The variables are very precise and

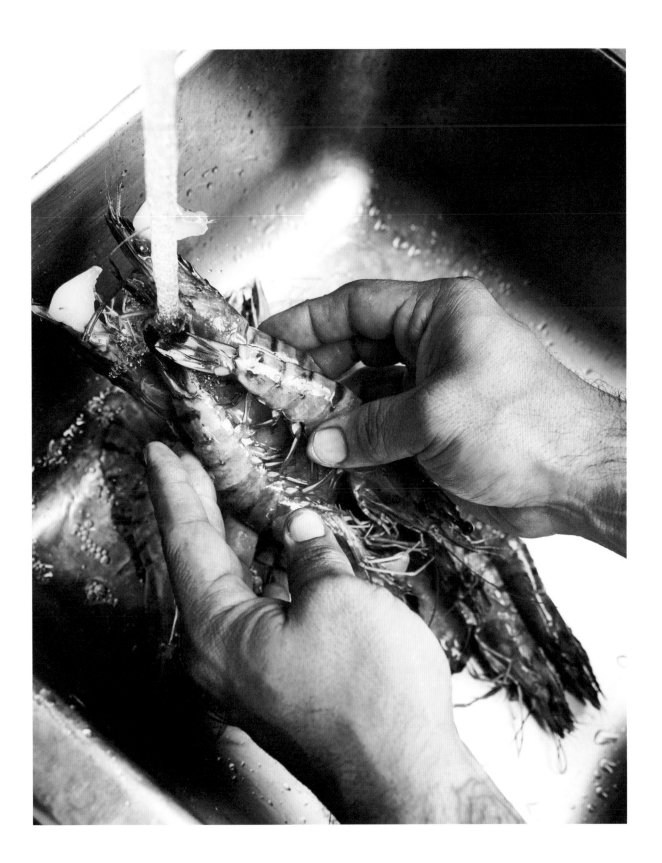

controllable. It's about getting the best ingredients, the perfect proportions, and putting it together in the right order. I'd make these brownies that were so high in fat and chocolate, they'd melt. Super-rich, super-heavy blocks of calories. I love baking. It's Zen. When I'm stressed, I like to bake.

But it was so Zen, it almost put me to sleep. It got boring. That's the life of a journeyman cook, you're never in one place very long, especially if you're not working for a chef who inspires you.

My next job was at Tortilla Jo's in Downtown Disney, working the garde-manger station, making salads and cold dishes. While I was working there, my car's transmission took a shit, and I had to take two buses to get down to Anaheim. It wasn't glamorous. It was alright but I still hadn't found my place. I was doing it mostly as a stepping stone. It was a Patina Group restaurant, which was good for the resume back then. But at that point, Patina had already become very corporate, and there wasn't the spirit of a chef behind it any more. It was just a business. Chefs who had come through Patina and made it what it was in its heyday had moved on to start their own restaurants— Walter Manzke and Gary Menes, whom I went on to work for, and David Meyer, Eric Greenspan, and Josiah Citrin.

Shortly after I started at Tortilla Jo's, Tanya pointed out an article in a food magazine about L'Auberge Carmel, a restaurant Walter Manzke had just opened in Carmel. I was, like, why am I working at a facsimile of a restaurant that used to be cool? I should work with the man himself. Me staying at Tortilla Joe's would be like joining a band that has a regular gig at a corporate convention center when what I really wanted to do was play for Charles Mingus or John Coltrane. Tanya booked us a reservation for that weekend.

We flew up to San Jose, rented a car, and drove to Carmel. Carmel is an idyllic little beach town on the Central Coast of California. It's foggy and beautiful, the coast is lined with cyprus trees and Tudor-style houses. Doris Day lives there and so does Clint Eastwood, who used to be the mayor. At the edge of the valley are rolling hills and farmland.

Honestly my first reaction to Carmel was, what the fuck? It's so small and quiet and rainy and cold. It looked strange to a kid from L.A. It didn't look like the California I knew.

But then we got to the restaurant and walked in the door. I'd never been in a place like that before. It was flawless. Dimly lit, just a handful of seats. We were also the youngest people in there by at least half—I was twenty-five at the time. The room was quiet and intimate but with the whirring, nonstop activity of a finely made watch. It offered a tasting menu, which was the first tasting menu I'd ever had. Every dish was intricate and perfect. I immediately fell in love.

Our dinner that night started with twelve elegantly crafted amuse-bouches. We were bombarded with flavors. Just one sip, or one bite, of something incredible and mind-blowing. Like the "lobster taco." I was expecting a . . . lobster taco. But what came out was a shot glass of tomato water, a chip, and a little spoon cradling about a half ounce of avocado mousse and a small piece of poached lobster. You eat it all together, and it tastes like a lobster taco.

The chef made a niçoise salad. It had everything you'd expect in a niçoise: tomatoes, green beans, olives, cucumbers, anchovy, rouille, ahi tuna, egg. But instead of a big giant salad, which is how you normally think of it, this is how Walter did it. First there was puréed heirloom tomato. It fills the whole plate to the rim, then four cubes of tuna were laid on top of that at right angles to the sides of the plate. Stacked on top of the tuna was a single green bean, a single anchovy, raw halved cherry tomatoes, a tiny quail egg, razor-thin cucumber slices, torn chervil, and a piece of toast smeared with rouille. A dash of grassy finishing olive oil, piment d'espelette, and sherry vinegar over everything. Then he put a shot of hot bouillabaisse on the side. Incredible.

What was obvious is that it was his own interpretation, his vision. Some of the techniques were French and some of the courses took inspiration from classic dishes, but it was always Walter's own take. I didn't really know about fine dining before that. We were naive students. It's like, you want to work at some Michelin-starred restaurant or temple of gastronomy because you've heard of it, but actually you don't know why you want to work there, and really, if you interrogate that impulse, you realize it's more about the resume. But when you eat at a place like L'Auberge, you get what the fuss is about. It was so delicious and different from anything I'd had.

At the end of the meal, I have to admit, I was still a little hungry. Premonition of what was to come for me I guess, a fat kid who fell in love with fine dining but ended up becoming a taco chef because, after it all, I always wanted to eat fatty delicious food. But as I remember it, the portions at L'Auberge were still pretty small that night, and they got bigger over the next year or two. Like I said, I eat like a pig.

We went back after the meal to meet the chef. The kitchen looked like it had been broken down for hours. It was like going into your grandmother's china room. Everybody was moving around the kitchen, silently. It didn't even smell like food in

there. There was no chopping. All the herbs were picked and the meat was portioned during prep. Everybody was in chef whites and carrying little spoons for tasters. You could have heard a pin drop. What I heard was the squeak of clogs and the "swish swish" of heavy canvas aprons. Very different from the raucous kitchens I'd worked in up to that point.

It was obvious who Walter was. There was an energy around him, and everybody was looking to him for guidance. He had these huge hands he'd use to gesture or grab things quickly, but always very smoothly. He talked with his hands, too, gesticulating to illustrate his point. He has a huge smile, and there's something kind of goofy about him, but he is very stoic.

He introduced himself. He was, like, "Hey dude, did you enjoy your meal?" Walter has a very deep voice and although he's not a surfer, he is from San Diego so he kind of talks like that. We complimented the meal and I told him I was a cook in L.A. He said we should hang out.

Almost immediately the kitchen went back to near-silence. Work was continuing and nobody was saying a word. And then, like a surgeon calling for his scalpel, I heard a big, booming voice: "Fire the squab." It was Walter. He spoke and immediately the place came alive. But alive, like, to the sound of a half-dozen spoons emulsifying sauces, the sizzle of a single portion of protein being grilled, maybe the tinkle of a plate being set down on the pass. Everybody was in sync, totally focused; nothing was over the top and showy. It was all about the precise technique that creates this beautiful food. It was kind of like a dance and very beautiful to watch.

I was, like, this is it. This is what I want to do! This is the real chef's work, happening in this tiny kitchen in a foggy coastal town halfway to Oregon.

Soon after, I returned to Carmel to stage for a night. And at the end of that night, I told Walter I'd like to work for him. He told me come back the next month. And that's how I came to move to Carmel and work for Walter for the next year-plus.

I didn't even know how much I was going to be paid. If I was going to be paid. After two weeks in the kitchen, I got a check for something like $800. He was paying me $10 an hour. I was stoked—I was, like, I don't have to get a second job! I started taking easy courses at the local community college on days off in order to get a deferral on my student loans.

I quickly learned that if you want to make it in fine dining, you have to give it everything. No dog, no girlfriend, no wife, no sports team, no kids, no friends, no nothing—except your brigade. And lucky for me, I didn't have any of these things in Carmel. So I was making it in fine dining when I was working at L'Auberge.

When I got the job, it was very last minute, and Tanya was in grad school, so there was no chance of her coming with me. I rented a room in a huge Spanish colonial–style house owned by a doctor who traveled all the time. I saw her maybe five times when I lived up there.

Carmel Valley is dead. Beautiful, but dead. There's maybe ten shops and one pub. The house I was living in was on top of a hill at the edge of town. It was so quiet. Too quiet. I'm used to falling asleep to the sound of dogs barking, the hum of the freeway, people yelling, constant car alarms, and the occasional gunshot. All I could hear in that house was the high-pitched screech of my inner ears going deaf from too many years of DJing and shows.

But I loved what I was doing. What Walter was doing at L'Auberge was what we call "temple level"—Michelin Star level—cooking. Up there with the French Laundry, Providence, and all that. And that was the trajectory I saw myself on.

I would count peanuts before plating them. Peanuts. And you know what? One night, Walter challenged me on the peanuts! He thought there were too many in there. But I dumped them out and counted them. There were sixteen, just like there was supposed to be. That's the wavelength you're on in a kitchen like that. Everybody has to be totally locked-in all the time.

One night, Walter was caught up with a purveyor and not in the kitchen when it came time to break down the fish we were serving. It was a beautiful hamachi. Everything else was ready and we were coming up on service. And usually nobody broke down the fish but Walter. But he was nowhere to be found, and there was going to be a roomful of people, who paid $300 a person, waiting on their fish.

I decided to break it down myself. I'd seen him do it a million times. Of course, I fucked up. Just ruined it. It doesn't matter how many times you've watched it happen, breaking down a huge, whole, scaly, slippery fish is super-hard to do, and your first time out you're more likely than not to fuck it up.

Walter came back and saw what I'd done. He was, like, "Dude. What the FUCK. Do NOT touch fish in my kitchen ever again." I'd never seen him raise his voice before. I watched sheepishly from the garde-manger station as he salvaged what he could of the hamachi. He made it into a sashimi and somehow saved most of it.

That was the worst I've ever felt in a kitchen. It's also one of the greatest lessons I've learned. Being less than perfect is both inevitable and unacceptable. You just have to keep learning, keep pushing yourself.

I was moving around the stations at L'Auberge, doing all the different jobs. I was trusted. It was a beautiful, small team—like Mingus's band. Every night, we killed it. And we all counted on each other.

But I knew L'Auberge wasn't going to last forever. I was getting homesick. And I guess I was missing something that I realized a little later is too important to me to give up for any kind of culinary success or stardom, which is a life. I now know that I don't want to be a Michelin-star chef. I just want to be me, do my food, love my wife and dog, go to sports games, eat out at other restaurants, and spend time with my family. It was the right time to move back to L.A., and besides, there were a few really great, fine dining restaurants there I could work at now that I'd spent the time at L'Auberge. When we said good-bye, Walter gave me a hug and told me I'd always have a job with him. (He later came to my wedding and I still consider him a dear friend.)

But when I came back to L.A., it was a reality check. I staged at all the fine dining restaurants in town—Providence, Melisse, Ortolan. These have much bigger kitchen brigades than what I saw at L'Auberge. I missed the intimacy of working with a small, tight-knit crew and the focused vision of a small restaurant.

Plus, I was making $10 an hour at L'Auberge, and this move was supposed to be a step up for me. But the fine dining restaurants in L.A. are much bigger kitchens so you're doing less-cool stuff, and you're still paid shit. Or, I guess, worse than shit. Providence offered me a job that paid $9.75. I had deferred my student loans while in Carmel. The whole point was moving on, paying down my debts, and advancing. I decided to take a job at the Palos Verdes Country Club that paid $15 an hour.

I loved working at the country club. I had total freedom. The normal country club fare like sand dabs and prime rib cart was expected, but we'd run specials. All we had to do there was break even in the kitchen. I was in charge of the fish station and I could buy whatever I wanted for specials. I did Normandy butter-poached halibut with pea tendrils and barley. But I did non-seafood specials, too. Sous-vide short ribs. Pork stomach stuffed with fish and vegetables from La Roux or chicken with black truffles under the skin. I was doing cool chef-y stuff and being paid decently to do it.

Of course, the first thing I did when I got to the country club was order me twelve hamachi, whole. I didn't want to get yelled at in a kitchen ever again. By number five or six, I was breaking them down lightning fast with no problem. That was a very quiet victory.

The country club had a scholarship program and they paid for me to go to Mexico and to France, where I studied at the Alain Ducasse school. I also went to Spain on my honeymoon. I came back from each of these trips with tons of new ideas, and the chef I was working for always supported whatever I wanted to do.

The hours were relatively chill. I'd moonlight at Palate Food + Wine and Marché. I was getting to know Gary Menes, the chef at Palate Food + Wine who would go on to run Le Comptoir. He would become a huge influence and mentor.

I was secure at the country club. I could have stayed forever in theory. But it wasn't quite enough. When Gary started Le Comptoir, I quit the country club to go work for him. That was a big moment. Gary pushed me to become a much better cook.

Le Comptoir had a chef-driven tasting menu, but was not, necessarily, striving to be a temple. Menes was a guy who wanted to make very good food his way. I was hired as sous chef.

Everything was vegetable-driven, another thing that I loved. We did a plate with seventeen or eighteen different vegetables on it. It was insane. I guess I was still basically a fat kid who couldn't imagine a meat-free dish giving him so much pleasure, but that kind of blew my mind. This dish had pickled onion, grilled eggplant, braised carrots, turnip, parsnip, roasted leek, roasted pear, roasted fennel, fried broccolini, and on and on. It came with a brightly colored sauce made with orange zest. That's where I learned root-to-flower cooking. If we got a bunch of parsley, we'd use the herb itself in one dish, and we'd pickle the roots to use in a different dish. If we got a pumpkin, we'd maybe make a soup with the flesh and then we'd roast the seeds and sprinkle them on top.

I guess as an antidote to all the precious vegetable dishes we were doing there, when we made staff meal, it was always rich comfort food. Gary would make these amazing pizzas with the sourdough starter we used. They were just so good. I still think he should open a pizzeria. It'd be the best in L.A. He'd crush. *Crush*. Gary, your pizzas are better than anybody's in town. Do it!

When it was my turn to do staff meal, I'd do tacos. The guys liked them. I'd get all the scraps of meat—wagyu beef, prime rib, or chicken—and I'd make a spice mix with onion powder, guajillo chile, clove, garlic powder, throw it all in the immersion circulator to cook it slow and low, sous-vide style. Then I'd crisp it up on the plancha. We'd eat tacos after service and drink wine leftover from the wine pairing. We ate good staff meals at Le Comptoir.

I was happy, but once again finances started to affect things. We did only four dinners a week. There just weren't enough shifts. At this point I was back to not paying my loans, but this time, it wasn't a deferral, I was on forbearance. I needed to make more money. To be honest I was stressed the fuck out about the debt and how I'd move on from this hand-to-mouth existence.

Back then nobody was doing "dressed up" or "fancy" tacos. Of course, tacos are everywhere in L.A. Really, *everywhere*—restaurants, driveways, drive-thrus, church parking lots, backyards, front yards. Tacos come in plastic bags, on paper plates, they come frozen in a box. Taco trucks are everywhere. And everybody has an opinion on what's the best taco around. But I didn't just want to do tacos. I wanted to do something completely different and unheard of. Something that combined my interests and experience as a cook in these finer restaurants with my upbringing and my fat-kid soul.

It was around this time that I started talking myself up at parties, when I saw chefs and fellow cooks around town, when I was drunk. I kept saying this ridiculous statement. This thing that is such a laughable idea. And people would laugh in my face when I said it. I see why. Because it's insane to say it. But I believed it. So I kept saying it.

"I'm going to open the best taco place in L.A."

EGGPLANT TACO

I love Greek food. There's a lot of eggplant in a Greek diet and also a lot of fried cheese. So I put these two things, my favorite parts of the Greek menu, together in a taco. It's great. If you can't find Japanese eggplants, and your eggplants are bigger or longer, you can cut them into bite-size pieces

2 pounds baby or Japanese eggplants, about 3 inches long, stemmed and halved lengthwise

Kosher salt

¼ cup extra-virgin olive oil

1 teaspoon freshly ground black pepper

8 or 9 thyme sprigs

6 garlic cloves, peeled and rough chopped

1 cup hazelnuts

3 tablespoons unsalted butter

8 ounces halloumi cheese, cut into 4-by-½-inch pieces

8 corn tortillas, warmed (see page 29)

Roasted Tomato Salsa (page 139) for serving

1 cup fresh flat-leaf parsley leaves torn from stems

1 lemon, halved

Preheat the oven to 375°F.

Season the eggplants with 1 tablespoon salt and let stand, cut-side up, for 10 minutes—until the bitterness goes away. Wipe off any moisture with a paper towel.

Brush the eggplants with the olive oil—the eggplants soak it up when they're roasting—and lay them in a roasting pan, cut-side up. Sprinkle with salt and the pepper and add the thyme and garlic.

Roast the eggplants for about 20 minutes, uncovered, until just cooked through.

Meanwhile, place the hazelnuts in a single layer on a rimmed baking sheet. Place in the oven and toast for 8 minutes, giving them a good shake halfway through. Remove from the oven and transfer to a food processor. Pulse once or twice—or, use the back of a knife to crush the nuts on a cutting board.

Remove the eggplants from the oven. Discard the garlic and thyme, then slice the eggplants into 1-inch coins. (If you have already cut into bite-size pieces, leave as is.)

In a 12-inch cast-iron skillet over medium heat, melt 2 tablespoons of the butter. Add the eggplants and sauté, cut-side down, until golden brown. Set aside in the skillet so they stay hot.

In a nonstick pan over medium-high heat, melt the remaining 1 tablespoon butter. Add the cheese and cook until golden brown on one side, about 1½ minutes. Flip them and leave in the pan until you're ready to plate.

Place one piece of cheese on each tortilla, add three or four eggplant pieces, some salsa, hazelnuts, and parsley. Finish with a squeeze of lemon juice. Serve immediately.

MUSHROOM TACO

Back when I was living in Carmel and working at L'Auberge, there was this old guy with a big beard who'd come into the restaurant with boxes of foraged porcinis or chanterelles. He'd sell them to us for $5 a pound, then he'd get the tasting menu.

I decided to go foraging. Just looking for some of the stuff we'd use at the restaurant. Miner's lettuce, wild asparagus, hazelnuts, and the most-prized foraged ingredient—wild mushrooms. It rains a lot there, so mushrooms are abundant. Porcini, elephant ears, candy caps. You can make ice cream out of candy caps. Mushrooms are amazing.

The day after it rains is the time to forage for mushrooms. So I mentioned my plan to my roommate, and she was, like, "There are mushrooms growing right out in front of the house!" I went out there and harvested 6 pounds of elephant ear mushrooms that day. Beginner's luck.

When available, I suggest using porcinis (in October in California), morels in the spring, but chanterelles, hedgehogs, hen of the woods (available in the spring and fall), portobellos, or oyster mushrooms, or shiitakes, or really any other cultivated mushroom available throughout the year will do. Even button mushrooms, and that's what we're using here. Ah, I love mushrooms.

We use a dense, dry Greek cheese with this. And don't be intimidated by the curry—you won't even taste the curry. It just adds to the umami blast of the mushrooms.

The salsa I copped from somewhere, I can't remember where though. Some Middle Eastern place. Lebanese coriander with oil and a little habanero. Just great.

To make the aleppo-habanero salsa: In a 10-inch cast-iron skillet over medium-low heat, combine the coriander seeds with 1 tablespoon of the olive oil and cook until aromatic, about 3 minutes.

Crush the garlic—just smash the cloves into a cutting board with the back of a knife, leaving them basically whole, but slightly broken, so the flavor can escape—and cook in the same pan with the coriander until aromatic, about 1½ minutes. Remove the pan from the heat.

continued

Aleppo-Habanero Salsa

¼ cup coriander seeds

½ cup extra-virgin olive oil

3 garlic cloves

2 tablespoons sherry vinegar, or to taste

2 tablespoons crushed Aleppo pepper or 1 tablespoon each dried red pepper flakes and paprika

1 habanero chile, stemmed

Kosher salt

6 tablespoons unsalted butter

1 pound shiitake mushrooms, stemmed and sliced paper-thin

2 garlic cloves, pierced with a knife

2 bay leaves

6 thyme sprigs

Kosher salt

Freshly ground black pepper

2 pounds button mushrooms, quartered

1 tablespoon curry powder

1 cup thinly sliced shallots

1 pound halloumi cheese, sliced into ½-inch-thick pieces about the length of an index finger

8 corn tortillas, warmed (see page 29)

1 cup fresh flat-leaf parsley leaves torn from stems

Using a wooden spoon, slide the contents of the pan into a blender and add the remaining 7 tablespoons olive oil, the vinegar, Aleppo pepper, and habanero. Blend on high speed until smooth and the coriander seeds are small enough to be hardly noticeable to the tooth. Taste and season with salt and more vinegar as you wish. Set aside in a warm place.

In a skillet over medium-high heat, warm 2 tablespoons of the butter. Add the shiitakes in an even layer and cook for 5 minutes, stirring occasionally. In these first 5 minutes you're losing moisture and also softening the mushrooms. Then add 1 garlic clove, 1 bay leaf, and 3 thyme sprigs. Cook for another 4 to 5 minutes, or until the mushrooms are caramelized and a little crispy. You want the texture of bacon. Crispy but not burned. Season with salt and pepper. Transfer to a plate and set aside in a warm place.

In the same pan, over medium-high heat, combine 3 tablespoons butter and the button mushrooms. Sauté them the exact same way, except, after they're coated in butter initially, add the curry powder and remaining garlic, bay leaf, and thyme. The mushrooms should cook faster, perhaps 6 minutes total to get them spongy and a little crispy and caramelized. When they're almost done, add the shallots and continue cooking until the shallots turn translucent. Season with salt and pepper. Set aside in a warm place.

In a 10-inch cast-iron skillet over medium heat, melt the remaining 1 tablespoon butter. Put the cheese directly in the pan and cook until golden brown, about 30 seconds per side. Don't move it around or anything. It won't stick. Don't worry.

Once the cheese is golden brown on the bottom, use a spatula to move it from the skillet to the tortillas, then add the button mushrooms, shiitakes, parsley, and salsa. Serve immediately.

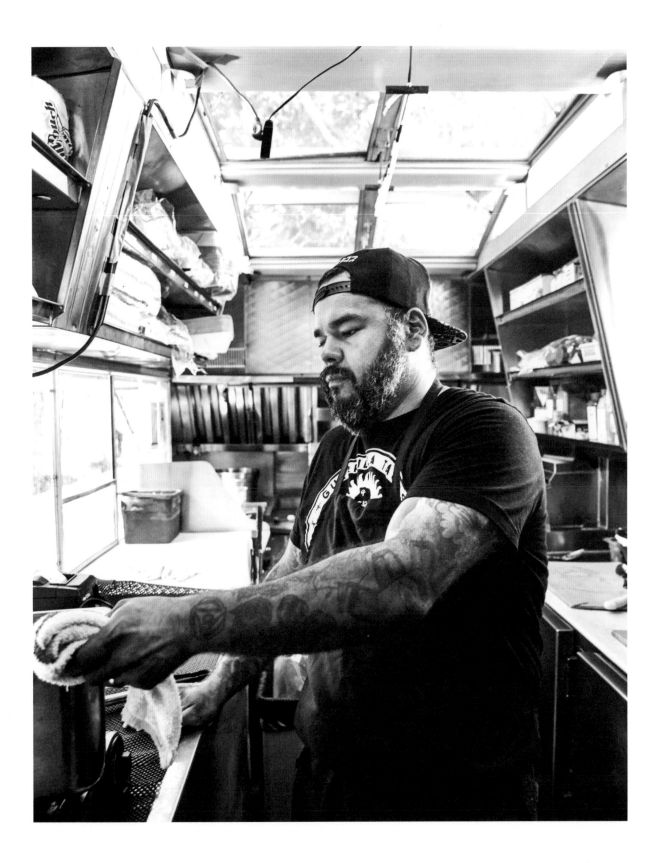

MUSHROOM ESCABECHE TACO

When we have wild mushrooms left over, we use them for escabeche. It is a tasty way of extending the shelf life of the mushrooms and a fun condiment for your fridge; here, we're making a nice egg-y taco with it. Clean the mushrooms very, very well—especially if you're using wild mushrooms. They're dirty.

Fill the sink with 6 inches of cold water. Add all the mushrooms and push them around, rubbing off the dirt and impurities with your fingers. The dirt should sink to the bottom, the mushrooms should bob to the top. Pick up the mushrooms with your hands, drain and clean the sink, and then rinse the mushrooms one more time under running water. Repeat this process a second time. Set the mushrooms on a wire rack. Slice the porcinis into 1-inch pieces. Cut the stems off the morels. Keep the chanterelles whole, but trim the bottoms.

In a deep 10-inch sauté pan over medium heat, warm 2 tablespoons of the olive oil. Add all the mushrooms, the garlic, thyme, rosemary, bay leaves, orange zest, chiles, peppercorns, vinegar, and 1 table-spoon of the salt and sauté for 3 minutes, or until the moisture starts to bubble a bit. Add the remaining olive oil, turn the heat to low, and let the mushrooms cook until softened, about 15 minutes. Season with the remaining 1 tablespoon salt and then turn off the heat. Transfer the mushrooms and liquid to a large mason jar, cover, and let the escabeche rest in the fridge for 1 day.

In a 10-inch cast-iron skillet over medium heat, warm all the mushrooms and liquid, about 2 minutes. Turn off the heat and let the mushrooms sit until you're ready to serve.

In a large, nonstick pan over medium-low heat, melt the butter. Add the eggs and, using a rubber spatula, stir constantly so they're totally mixed and not sticking to the pan. When the eggs are still slightly runny, remove the pan from the heat and keep stirring. When the eggs are just set, leave them alone.

Distribute the eggs among the tortillas. Then, add 3 tablespoons escabeche to each and garnish with the salsa. Serve immediately.

8 ounces porcini mushrooms

8 ounces morel mushrooms

8 ounces chanterelle mushrooms

2 cups extra-virgin olive oil

6 garlic cloves, peeled and crushed with the side of a knife

3 thyme sprigs

1 rosemary sprig

2 bay leaves

Zest of 1 orange

2 dried chiles de árbol

8 peppercorns

1 cup red wine vinegar

2 tablespoons kosher salt

3 tablespoons butter

6 eggs

6 corn tortillas, warmed (see page 29)

Raw Chile-Garlic Salsa (page 127) for garnishing

STUFFED SQUASH BLOSSOM TACO

The crunch of the battered squash and the slightly sweet richness of this filling make a great taco. Try to get the freshest squash blossoms possible because if they're slightly wilted it is difficult to stuff them and maintain their shape. If you can get blossoms, you can probably get heirloom tomatoes, so pair it with this fresh tomato salsa.

To make the heirloom tomato salsa: In a food processor, gently pulse the tomatoes into a thick puree. Add the jalapeño, garlic, olive oil, and vinegar and pulse on high speed for 40 seconds. Season with salt and pepper. Set aside.

To make the stuffed squash blossoms: Trim the stems from the blossoms and set the blossoms aside. As much as possible, maintain the shape of the blossoms—they're going to be holding a lot of cheese and you want them to keep their shape.

In a bowl, using a fork, whip together all the cheeses until smooth. Add the shallots, parsley, and 1½ teaspoons of the salt; season with pepper; and stir until evenly distributed. Scoop the cheese filling into a large ziplock bag. Cut off the corner from one edge of the bag. Twisting the other end of the bag, squeeze the filling into the blossoms until they are full. Close the petals around the filling.

In a large bowl, sift together the all-purpose flour, rice flour, baking powder, and remaining 1 teaspoon salt. In another bowl, whisk together the egg and seltzer until stiff. Then, stir the egg mixture into the flour mixture, keeping the batter slightly chunky.

In a deep pot over high heat, bring 2 to 3 inches of vegetable oil to 360°F. Test by adding ½ tablespoon batter to the oil—it should bubble and puff up slightly and turn golden brown in 2 minutes.

Dredge the blossoms gently in the batter, then add to the hot oil, five or six at a time or as many as will fit without crowding the pan, and fry until golden brown, about 4 minutes.

Place two stuffed blossoms on each tortilla, add some salsa and then the chives. Serve immediately.

Heirloom Tomato Salsa

2 cups rough-cut heirloom tomatoes, any variety

1 jalapeño chile, stemmed

2 garlic cloves, peeled

¼ cup extra-virgin olive oil

2 tablespoons sherry vinegar

Kosher salt

Freshly ground black pepper

Stuffed Squash Blossoms

18 squash blossoms

1 cup ricotta

1 cup mascarpone

1 cup queso fresco

1 to 2 shallots, minced

1 cup very finely minced parsley

2½ teaspoons kosher salt

Freshly ground black pepper

1 cup unbleached all-purpose flour

1 cup rice flour

2 teaspoons baking powder

1 egg

⅔ cup very cold seltzer water

Vegetable oil or lard for frying

9 corn tortillas, warmed (see page 29)

2 tablespoons minced fresh chives, or parsley

CAULIFLOWER TACO

I don't remember why we started doing cauliflower tacos, but it just works. You don't want the cauliflower mushy, it should be more crispy and browned and a little bit caramelized. You're looking for some crunch from the pine nuts, some sweetness from the dates, and some sourness from the olives and salsa. I like to use Romanesco, or bright orange or purple cauliflower, for color, but you can use whatever is available.

Kosher salt

1 head of cauliflower or Romanesco, stems and leaves removed, cut into bite-size florets

¼ cup pine nuts

2 tablespoons unsalted butter

2 garlic cloves, peeled and smashed with the side of a knife

1 teaspoon curry powder

4 thyme sprigs

1 cup Medjool dates, seeded and sliced into edible pieces

Freshly ground black pepper

12 corn tortillas, warmed (see page 29)

1 cup Castelvetrano olives, pitted and quartered

Roasted Tomato Salsa (page 139) for topping

5 leaves fresh fenugreek or parsley, roughly torn from stem

Fill a large stockpot with about 4 quarts water. Add salt until it's as salty as the sea. Set over high heat and bring to a boil. Add the cauliflower to parboil and then remove after 3 to 4 minutes, when the cauliflower is about three-quarters done. Drain completely.

Meanwhile, in a dry pan over medium heat, toast the pine nuts just until slightly fragrant, about 4 minutes. Remove from the heat and set aside.

In a 10-inch cast-iron skillet over medium-high heat, melt the butter. Add the cauliflower florets and cook for 2 to 3 minutes, or until they start turning golden brown. Add the garlic, curry powder, and thyme and continue to cook until the florets are fully golden brown and crispy in places, about 10 minutes. Add the dates and pine nuts and toss with the cauliflower. Season with salt and pepper. Remove from the heat and discard the garlic and thyme.

Add the cauliflower mixture to the tortillas, then the olives, top with some salsa, and finish with the fenugreek. Serve immediately.

SERVES 6 (2 TACOS EACH)

CHICKEN ADOBO TACO

The idea for this recipe comes from a family meal we would have at L'Auberge Carmel. The pastry chef, Margarita Manzke, would make this dish, and I asked her to show me how to make it and I absorbed the knowledge like a sponge. Whenever I do make this for family meal, people can't get enough of it. This is also really good served with white rice if you don't have tortillas around.

8 boneless, skinless chicken thighs

1 cup white vinegar

½ cup soy sauce

1 head of garlic, peeled and thinly sliced

8 thyme sprigs

8 dried chiles de árbol

6 bay leaves

20 black peppercorns

1 cinnamon stick

12 corn tortillas, warmed (see page 29)

Avocado-Tomatillo Salsa (page 76) for garnishing

1 bunch of scallions, ends removed, white parts cut into 1-inch pieces, green parts very thinly sliced

In a pot over medium-low heat, combine the chicken, vinegar, soy sauce, garlic, thyme, chiles, bay leaves, peppercorns, and cinnamon and simmer until the chicken is well glazed, about 1½ hours.

Remove the chicken from the mixture, debone and cut into thick slices, and then return to the sauce. Turn the heat to low to keep it warm.

Spoon the chicken and sauce onto the tortillas. Garnish with the salsa and a lot of scallions. Serve immediately.

GROUPER TACO

When I first encountered fish poached in butter or olive oil at L'Auberge, I loved it. It enhances the richness of the fish by slowly bringing up the heat and keeping the consistency moist. It's the perfect for texture for fish in a taco.

To make the raw chile-garlic salsa: In a blender or food processor, combine the padróns, cayennes, Fresnos, habaneros, garlic, and olive oil. Blend on medium-low speed or pulse until chunky. Mix in the vinegar and season with salt. It should be spicy, garlic-y, colorful. Set aside.

To make the spinach-potato puree: Select a large (4-quart) heavy stockpot to cook in. Then, get a piece of wax paper in the shape of a square and fold it in half. Fold it in half a second time to make a square again. Fold that square on a diagonal so that the loose ends of the paper form the top of the triangle. Fold that triangle again, lengthwise, to form a skinnier triangle, and then fold once more to form an even skinnier triangle. Now take the triangle over to your pot and, placing the small end of the triangle at the center of the pot, grab the other end where it meets the pot's lid. Trim the large end of the triangle to that length and snip a little off the skinny end of the triangle. Open it up—it should be a circle the size and shape of your pot, with a hole in the middle. This is a cartouche.

Remove the green part and root from the leeks. Dice the white and give it a cold water bath to remove all the dirt. Remove from the water and drain.

In that 4-quart stockpot over medium-low heat, melt the butter. Add the leek and sauté until translucent, about 10 minutes. Add the potatoes and gently cook for 3 to 4 minutes. When the potatoes are lightly sautéed, add the 1½ cups heavy cream, enough to cover the potatoes and leek by about three-fourths. Now cover your pot with your cartouche. You want it to loosely cover the potatoes. Cook for

continued

Raw Chile-Garlic Salsa

4 padrón peppers

4 cayenne chiles

2 Fresno chiles

2 habanero chiles

3 garlic cloves, peeled and chopped

1 cup extra-virgin olive oil

½ cup white vinegar

Kosher salt

Spinach-Potato Puree

1 leek

2 tablespoons unsalted butter

2 Yukon gold potatoes, cut into 1-by-1-inch cubes

1½ cups heavy cream, plus 2 tablespoons

Kosher salt

6 cups tightly packed spinach

Freshly ground black pepper

3 pounds unsalted butter

2 pounds grouper fillet, divided into 2½-ounce portions (see Note, page 129)

Kosher salt

Freshly ground black pepper

12 corn tortillas, warmed (see page 29)

2 lemons, halved

Minced fresh chives for garnishing

20 to 30 minutes, or until potatoes are soft; use a wooden spoon to stir it every once in a while. You want *no color whatsoever* on the potatoes. The cream will reduce a little bit and be absorbed into the potato. After 30 minutes, remove from the heat and set aside.

Prepare an ice-water bath in the largest mixing bowl you have by stirring together water and a tray of ice.

Half fill an 8-quart pot with water and set over high heat. Once the water is boiling, season with salt, and add all the spinach. Wilt the spinach down until it is bright green and cooked, maybe 30 to 45 seconds. Transfer the spinach to the ice-water bath to stop the cooking. Remove from the bath and place in a strainer. Put pressure on the spinach, with a spatula or large spoon, and squeeze out the water. Place the spinach in a blender, blend on medium speed, and add the remaining 2 tablespoons heavy cream, until it's blending well. Then add the potatoes and blend until the puree is a beautiful bright green. Use a spoon to scrape bigger chunks off the sides. The consistency should be a thicker whipped mashed potato. Season with salt and pepper. Put the puree in a pot and set aside.

In a 10-inch cast-iron skillet over medium to medium-low heat, warm the butter to 180° to 190°F. Season the fish well with salt and pepper. Working in batches, add the fish, maybe three or four pieces at a time, to the skillet and gently poach until cooked through, 3 to 4 minutes. Gently lift the fish off the bottom of the pan so it doesn't stick or fall apart. Once cooked, transfer the fish to a metal grate to drain. (When you're on your last batch of fish, that's when you start to warm up your tortillas.)

Spread about 1 tablespoon spinach puree on each tortilla; then add the fish, a squeeze of lemon juice, and some salsa; and garnish with chives. Serve immediately.

NOTE If you can't find grouper, you can use the same amount of sea bass or other white fish.

SHRIMP AND CHORIZO TACO

Two of my favorite things while I was growing up were chorizo and shrimp. Here, we put them together for a very simple lunchtime taco. This goes great with a shot or two of mezcal. Or maybe three . . .

1 pound U16 shrimp

8 ounces chorizo (see page 54)

½ cup cherry tomatoes, halved lengthwise

Kosher salt

Freshly ground black pepper

6 corn tortillas, warmed (see page 29)

Raw Tomatillo Salsa (page 160) for topping

Using a paring knife, peel and devein the shrimp. Set aside.

In a 10-inch cast-iron skillet over medium-high heat, render the chorizo for 3 to 4 minutes, breaking it up with a wooden spoon as you go. Add the shrimp and let brown, about 2 minutes. Add the tomatoes and let blister, about 2 minutes. Season with salt and pepper.

Divide the shrimp and chorizo mixture evenly among the tortillas, then top with a healthy dose of salsa. Serve immediately.

TUNA POKE AND SEA URCHIN TOSTADA

I ate Ono Seafood's poke in Honolulu in 2013 and came back and started doing poke tostadas right away. That poke was one of the best things I have ever had. The white miso, the beautiful fish, with a few complementary spices . . . perfect for a tostada! We started doing this before fast-casual poke and the whole craze that's taken over L.A. People do poke now because it's trendy and an easy business model where you don't have to have a real kitchen and permitting for a hood. When we first served this, poke was still a strictly Hawaiian thing, or something cooks did in culinary school and then never did again. Now it's like the new kale. But we'll keep doing it. Because it's so good.

To make the salsa del valle: In a 10-inch cast-iron skillet over medium-high heat, warm 2 tablespoons of the olive oil. Add all the chiles and cook until toasty and burning your nostrils a bit on an inhale, about 2 minutes. They should turn a darkish brown color. Add the almonds, pine nuts, and garlic and cook for about 3 minutes, or until golden brown. Slide these ingredients into the blender. Add the vinegar and remaining 10 tablespoons olive oil and puree it to death—on high speed for about 5 minutes. Let cool, then season with kosher salt, add the cashews, and mix with a spoon. Set aside.

If you've got a loin, trim the bloodline (the darker part) and remove the skin. Lay the fish on a dampened kitchen towel and use a knife to pull off the dark matter and impurities. Flip the fish flesh-side down. On the top, make a small incision between the skin and the flesh. Use another towel to pinch the end so the fish doesn't slide off when you're removing the skin. Work the knife slowly away from you, pulling the skin up from the flesh. Discard the skin.

Dampen a kitchen towel and wipe a very sharp knife on both sides so it's clean and also a little wet—this will help it cut through the flesh cleanly. Using strong single strokes, cut the fish into 1½-inch cubes. Set aside.

In a bowl, vigorously whisk together the miso, soy sauce, yuzu juice, sesame oil, and olive oil. Fold in the tuna so it's completely coated. Season with furikake. Set the poke aside.

continued

Salsa del Valle

¾ cup extra-virgin olive oil

7 guajillo chiles, stemmed and seeded

6 chiles de árbol, stemmed and seeded

2 tablespoons blanched and slivered almonds

2 tablespoons pine nuts

4 garlic cloves, peeled and chopped

½ cup white vinegar

Kosher salt

½ cup roasted chopped cashews

2 pounds fresh tuna loin or steak (albacore, ahi, bigeye)

½ cup very good white miso (the most expensive kind is usually best)

¼ cup soy sauce

¼ cup yuzu juice

1 tablespoon sesame oil

1 tablespoon extra-virgin olive oil

Furikake for seasoning

¼ cup vegetable oil

8 corn tortillas

Kosher salt

2 live sea urchins, or 8 pieces (see Note)

½ cup thinly sliced scallions (white and green parts)

1 lime, halved

Sea salt

Several slices of cucumber for garnishing

Parsley for garnishing

Line a wire rack with paper towels.

In a 10-inch cast-iron skillet over medium-high heat, warm the vegetable oil to about 375°F. Add the tortillas and fry until crispy, about 30 seconds per side. Or, put the tortillas right over the flame of the range until they're blistering and dry. Season your tortillas with kosher salt after pulling them from the oil or fire. Let them cool on the prepared rack until they're slightly warmer than room temperature. (You can also buy tostada shells.)

In the meantime, prepare an ice-water bath in the largest mixing bowl you have by stirring together water and a tray of ice. Cover a plate with paper towels. Set both aside.

Wearing gloves, flip the sea urchins over onto a kitchen towel or a rimmed baking sheet, with the mouth facing up. Take a hard metal spoon in each hand, with the lips facing out—as if you're playing the spoons. Force one spoon into the hole. Tap down on it with the other spoon gingerly until you hear a crack. Then jam them both in and, working the spoons in a pruning-shear motion, crack open each sea urchin. It'll be messy, which is why you have it all laid out on a kitchen towel. Rinse your spoons and carefully scrape the yellow sea urchin roe away from the shell. There should be five portions. Take care not to break up the roe, each portion should come off in a piece, like a small, long tongue. Put these pieces into the ice-water bath to clean off any impurities. Set the sea urchin roe on the prepared plate and, using tweezers, remove any more impurities.

Place a layer of tuna poke on each tostada, then add salsa (as much as you want for how spicy you like it), scallions, one or two pieces of sea urchin roe, a sprinkle of furikake, and a squeeze of lime juice. I like to hit it with a pinch of sea salt at the end. Serve immediately.

NOTE Google! See if you can find live uni (sea urchin) in your area. Just get the nicest stuff from the best source. If you can't, Japanese markets will sell cleaned and shucked uni in 250- and 500-gram packets. You're looking for eight pieces or more.

MUSSEL QUESADILLA

I really enjoy eating mussels. It's a little bit of work getting the meat out of the shells, but it's worth it. Oaxacan cheese works really well here. Lemon adds a nice tartness but also a little sweetness that comes in with the preserving process.

To make the preserved lemons: Slice the lemons very thinly into rounds. Discard any pieces from the tops and bottoms that are only peel with no flesh.

In a large bowl, mix together the salt and the sugar. Layer half the salt mixture into a glass baking dish, then layer the lemon slices on top of one another and push them into the salt mixture. Cover the lemons with the remaining salt mixture and push the mixture into the lemons so it's all compacted. Wrap the dish in plastic wrap and pop into the freezer overnight. The next day, remove from the freezer and place in the fridge. Your lemons will be ready to use and will keep for up to 1 week.

In a pan over medium heat, cook the bacon until the fat is rendered off and the bacon is crispy, about 4 minutes. (Enjoy the smell of bacon cooking while you clean your mussels, removing the beard.)

In a 10-inch sauté pan over medium-high heat, warm the ¼ cup olive oil. Add the mussels and wine and bring to a rumbling boil. Add the shallots, garlic, thyme, and lemon juice and cover with a plate or pan lid. Turn the heat to high and cook for 4 to 6 minutes, until the mussel shells open. Remove the pan from the heat and discard any mussels that did not open—that means they came to you dead! Discard the garlic and thyme. Strain the liquid into a saucepan and set the mussels aside.

Bring the mussel liquid to a boil and then lower to a simmer, reducing it slightly. While the liquid is reducing, remove the mussels from their shells. When the liquid is reduced, about 10 minutes,

continued

Preserved Lemons

2 lemons, washed

1 cup kosher salt

1 cup sugar

8 ounces slab bacon, cut into 1-by-2-inch pieces

¼ cup extra-virgin olive oil, plus 2 tablespoons

2 pounds Prince Edward Island or other blue mussels, shells on

2 cups dry white wine

2 shallots, peeled and very thinly sliced

4 garlic cloves, peeled and smashed with the side of a knife

3 thyme sprigs

Juice of 1 lemon

4 tablespoons unsalted butter

Four 8-inch flour tortillas

8 ounces Oaxacan cheese, torn into ½-inch pieces

1 avocado, pitted, peeled, quartered lengthwise, and very thinly sliced

2 tablespoons dried red pepper flakes

1 cup fresh flat-leaf parsley leaves, torn from stems

¼ cup minced fresh chives, minced

remove the pan from the heat and return the mussels to the broth and allow to steep, about 5 minutes.

Rinse about 8 slices of the preserved lemons to remove excess salt and sugar brine and pat them dry.

In a sauté pan over medium heat, warm the 2 tablespoons olive oil. Add the rinsed preserved lemons and cook until slightly caramelized.

In a 10-inch cast-iron skillet over medium heat, warm 1 tablespoon of the butter until melted. Add a tortilla and cover with one-fourth of the Oaxacan cheese and allow to melt. Using a slotted spoon, add one-fourth of the mussels. Add one-fourth of the bacon bits as well, and fold the tortilla over onto itself. Cook until the tortilla is golden brown on both sides (when folded), about 45 seconds on each side. Repeat with the remaining butter, tortillas, and fillings. For a prettier quesadilla, you can also keep this open face.

Top each quesadilla with avocado, red pepper flakes, and preserved lemons, about three slices per quesadilla. Garnish with parsley and chives. Serve immediately.

ARTICHOKE QUESADILLA

When I worked at L'Auberge, I was living near the artichoke capital of the world, Castroville, which is about fifty miles up the road from Carmel on the way to Santa Cruz. At the restaurant, Walter would do a salad with artichokes seven different ways—puréed, fried, raw, braised. . . . My favorite was the fried baby artichokes. Artichokes are a lot of work in the kitchen. On days off, I'd go to a show in Santa Cruz or go drinking with friends up there, just blow off steam. Once we caught an Ozomatli show and ended up driving off the road into an artichoke field to poach a few plants. An artichoke is a very fibrous plant—as I found out that night while trying to remove the hearts with my bare hands—part of why they're tough to prepare. But baby artichokes are perfect for a quesadilla. The tomato confit can be prepared 1 day ahead.

To confit the tomatoes: Preheat the oven to 200°F. Line a baking sheet with aluminum foil.

Bring a half-filled 8-quart pot of salted water to a boil. Add the tomatoes one by one for 30 seconds each—just long enough that you can peel off the skin easily. Make sure the water stays at a boil. Using a paring knife, or a potato peeler, peel immediately. Quarter the tomatoes lengthwise and remove the seeds and pulpy core, which you can throw away or reserve for another use.

In a bowl, combine the tomatoes with the salt, sugar, olive oil, and thyme. Arrange the tomatoes in nice lines on the prepared baking sheet. Roast for 2 hours, then flip them and forget about them for another 2 hours. You want them soft and cooked-through, but not crispy. They should be fatty-feeling and almost melting.

To make the roasted tomato salsa: Prepare a medium fire in a charcoal grill or heat a gas grill to medium.

Put the whole tomatoes on the grill grate and roast until they're black on one side. Then, using tongs, turn the tomatoes to roast evenly. After about 5 minutes, add the onion and chiles. The tomatoes should turn very black, like black-black, almost to

continued

Tomato Confit

6 Roma tomatoes, tops removed and scored on the bottom with an X

1 tablespoon kosher salt

1½ teaspoons sugar

¼ cup extra-virgin olive oil

8 or 9 thyme sprigs

Roasted Tomato Salsa

4 Roma tomatoes

½ red onion

1 serrano chile, stemmed

1 jalapeño chile, stemmed

6 garlic cloves, peeled

¼ cup white vinegar

Kosher salt

Juice of 1 lemon

16 baby artichokes

4 cups vegetable oil

2 tablespoons extra-virgin olive oil

2 tablespoons sherry vinegar

2 tablespoons minced fresh chives

2 shallots, very thinly sliced

Kosher salt

Cracked black pepper

2 tablespoons butter

Six ½-inch-thick slices Oaxacan cheese

Six 8-inch flour tortillas

6 eggs

Parsley for garnishing

the point where they're getting gray, about 35 minutes. The chiles and onion should be somewhat charred.

In a food processor, combine the tomatoes, chiles, onion, garlic, and vinegar. Pulse; keeping it chunky and leave the seeds in there. Season with salt. Set aside.

Fill a pot with water and add the lemon juice. Peel the leaves from the artichokes until you reach the point where the leaves are pale-ish yellow. Remove the spiky ends of the leaves. Peel the stalks, cut in halves lengthwise, and trim each to about 2 inches. As you work, drop the artichokes into to the lemon water so they don't oxidize.

Pour the vegetable oil into a Dutch oven or a heavy pot and heat to 360° to 365°F. Remove the artichokes from the water and pat them dry. When the oil is hot—it should not be bubbling—drop in the artichokes, being careful not to crowd the pan too much. Fry the artichokes until they are golden brown, 4 to 6 minutes. Using a spider or slotted spoon, remove the artichokes and let the excess oil drip back into the pot. Transfer the fried artichokes to a bowl and toss with the olive oil, sherry vinegar, chives, and shallots and season with salt and pepper. Set aside on a grate or wire rack to drain until you're ready to assemble the quesadillas.

In a 10-inch cast-iron skillet over medium heat, warm 1 tablespoon of the butter. Put the sliced cheese into the skillet and fry until golden brown, about 2 minutes. They shouldn't be sticking.

Place the tortillas on top of the cheese until they stick, flip everything over, and let the tortillas cook until they're golden brown. You should be able to push them around as units.

When the tortillas and cheese are ready, remove from the pan and immediately add the remaining 1 tablespoon butter to the skillet. Turn the heat to medium-low, add an egg, and cook until the white sets. Season with salt and pepper and set aside. Repeat with the remaining eggs.

Top your tortilla and melted cheese with a few pieces of tomato confit, a layer of 'chokes, and an egg. Add as much salsa as you like and garnish with some parsley. These quesadillas should be served one at a time. Serve your favorite guest first and then keep cooking until everybody has a quesadilla.

BOUILLABAISSE

I used to make gallons of this at the country club. You can use any good white fish, basically any fish but oily, fatty fish—that means no salmon, mackerel, bluefish, tuna, and the like (when you're buying fish, get your fishmonger to butcher it for you and separate out the carcasses—freeze them until you're ready to make this stock, up to 3 months). The recipe makes more fish stock than you'll need. You can freeze whatever you don't use and make more bouillabaise throughout the month—that's how long I'd keep this stock in the freezer.

Fish Stock

2 leeks

One 750-ml bottle dry white white

3 pounds fish carcasses, from halibut, swordfish, any white fish

1 yellow onion, ends removed and rough chopped

4 garlic cloves, peeled and rough chopped

3 carrots, peeled and rough chopped

2 celery ribs, ends removed and rough chopped

1 bay leaf

5 peppercorns

1 whole clove

3 thyme sprigs

4 parsley sprigs

8 cups water, or as needed

To make the fish stock: Remove the green parts and roots from the leeks. Dice the whites and give them a cold water bath to remove all the dirt. Remove from the water and drain.

In a 10-quart stockpot over high heat, combine the wine, fish carcasses, onion, leeks, garlic, carrots, celery, bay leaf, peppercorns, clove, thyme, parsley, and enough of the water to cover the ingredients completely. Cook for 5 minutes, then add more water to cover the vegetables, if needed. Bring back to a boil and then turn the heat to medium-low. Simmer for 45 minutes and then strain, discarding the solids. You should have 3 to 4 quarts of stock; you'll need a quart for the stew. Transfer the rest to an airtight container and freeze for another use.

To make the tomato base: Core and chop the tomatoes. In a blender, combine the tomatoes, sherry vinegar, olive oil, garlic, and lemon juice and puree until very smooth. Season with salt. Set aside.

In a 4-quart stockpot over medium-high heat, combine 1 quart fish stock, 1 cup of the tomato base, and the halibut, opah, shrimp, mussels, and clams. Cook for about 4 minutes, or until the shells open. Turn the heat to medium-low and add another ¼ cup tomato base. You want that raw, bright tomato and garlic flavor. People dig it!

Season well with salt and pepper and sprinkle with parsley. Serve with ½ lemon for each person to squeeze on top, if desired, and some extremely crusty bread.

Tomato Base

5 Roma tomatoes, halved lengthwise

¼ cup sherry vinegar

¼ cup olive oil

2 garlic cloves, peeled

¼ cup fresh lemon juice

Kosher salt

3 ounces halibut, cut into large cubes

2 ounces opah (Hawaiian moon fish), cut into large cubes

2 (16/20 size) head-on shrimp (see headnote, page 176), peeled and deveined

6 mussels, Prince Edward Island or comparably large mussels

8 Manila clams

Kosher salt

Freshly ground black pepper

2 tablespoons chopped fresh flat-leaf parsley

1 lemon, halved (optional)

Crusty bread, toasted, for serving

THE CART + THE TRUCK

"Fancy" tacos born on the streets of L.A.

SO, I WAS GOING TO OPEN THE BEST TACO PLACE IN L.A.

But I had no idea how I'd get beyond where I was. I had no plan. The taco place was, like, something I was going to do in the future. Le Comptoir was a great place, even though I wasn't really making enough for me to get by. I still felt like I had a lot to learn as a cook.

In the meantime, my bank account just kept getting lower and lower. I was living check to check. That July, I had to borrow money from Tanya to pay rent. A few weeks later I looked at my bank account. I had $167 in checking. If I didn't make enough money in the next few weeks somehow, I was going to have to borrow money from her again to pay rent, or just to live. I knew she'd cover me, but that gets old after a while. I just didn't want to do that anymore.

I knew this guy, Tyler Wells. He'd come into the restaurant at bunch and we had struck up a friendship. He'd invited us to come check out the cafe where he worked, this brand-new third-wave coffee place called Handsome Coffee Roasters, in the Arts District east of downtown L.A. I was, like, "The Arts District? Nobody goes there." This was 2012. But he kept talking it up. Handsome had only been open a few months and was one of the first new businesses to open in the area that was basically a nowheresville of warehouses, film locations, and depots across the river from downtown.

Every Wednesday evening at Handsome, they'd bring produce back from the Santa Monica Farmers' Market and resell it at the cafe. I went one Wednesday. A couple dozen people who had started living in converted lofts around the Arts District or were super into coffee had made it a regular meet-up. People were drinking wine and beer on the street. It was a cool scene.

I called Tyler.

"Hey, do you mind if I set up a taco cart in front of Handsome this week?"

This was Tuesday at 4 p.m.

"Sure," Tyler said. "See you tomorrow."

I hung up the phone and started to laugh. I had no idea what I was doing.

I had a little hibachi grill. And I had bought a little propane cart with a griddle for a cook-out in a park a few months back, so I could use that to cook. The rest of it

I figured I could get at Super King Market. A bunch of chicken and beef and bulk amounts of tomatillos, some propane for the cart, spices for marinade—King has it all. It's the best market on the planet. I spent $143 at King buying supplies, leaving $24 in my checking account. But I had what I needed to make tacos.

I came back to my apartment and prepped all night for the next day. I called my friends and family and begged them to come out. Tanya was there, helping me mix and blend, chop and marinate. She said she'd come out and help work the cart, taking orders and dealing with customers. Gary Menes, my chef at Le Comptoir, told me he'd come to support.

My only goal was to make back the money I'd spent at Super King and maybe a little extra to get closer to being able to pay rent. I had no idea if I'd get there.

The Arts District was dead back then. It was known for . . . basically nothing. And there was definitely no food there then. Totally different from today, which is all boutiques and cafes and lofts, design firms and film production houses, and more coming in all the time. People don't film down there because there are more businesses and less shutting down of streets. You can't get those iconic shots of the bridges to downtown so much anymore. Parking is tougher now.

There's a picture of me cooking on the cart and the hibachi that first day. I'm wearing flipflops, manning the grill. It was the weirdest August weather—totally humid, stagnant air, very hot. Smoke everywhere. Gary ended up hopping behind the cart to help out, slicing up the chicken that came off the hibachi. I had neglected to get any to-go containers or napkins. Everything came out on paper plates and that was it. I didn't have any drinks. I didn't even have any cash in the till. I had to send Tanya to B of A in order to give people change.

Just looking at that photo makes my body ache. That set-up was so labor intensive. I had to keep refreshing the coals—throw the ash in the gutter and make sure it was totally extinguished while lighting another chimney of coals, while serving tacos as they were ordered, while making change, while talking people up, while cooking. It didn't make much sense and was much more chaotic than I'd anticipated.

But the food was good enough. And my friends and family came out, along with a few Arts District regulars who were at the market that first day. I made about $300. Doubled my investment. Not bad.

I decided to do it again the next week. And the next week. Gradually, things got more legit. I got a pop-up table and a tablecloth. I had change. And I bought some sodas

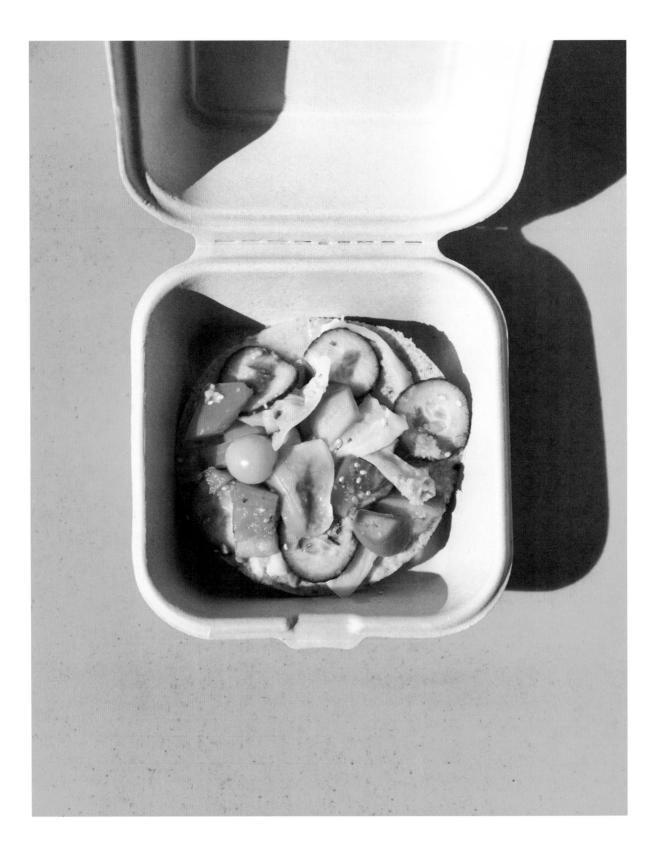

and napkins. The third or fourth week, I added a Square reader so people could use cards to pay for their tacos. More people were showing up, and the menu was growing. I added a potato and roasted corn taco, then started experimenting with other meats—lamb, ground boar, beautiful Cook Pig Ranch pork. And I started doing cauliflower and mushrooms, vegetarian and vegan stuff. The hibachi lasted for a few months at least. Fellow cooks seemed to admire that—cooking with coals on the street.

I was still working my regular shifts at Le Comptoir, but I was also doing what I really wanted to do—and making money I needed to pay my loans and rent on the side. I was happy.

That October we got a little write-up in the *LA Weekly*. Things got busier and busier. There'd be, like, twenty or thirty people around the cart at times, drinking beer and wine and eating tacos on the street. It was beautiful.

Soon, Handsome was going so well that I started cooking in front of Café Dulce, near the Staples Center in downtown L.A. I started using social media to blast out our menus and tell people where we were going to be. We got some regular customers. That month, I was able to make my rent money off of selling tacos! And as soon as I made rent money selling tacos, I knew it was time to quit Le Comptoir. But I never really quit, I just stopped working there. Gary was opening the permanent Le Comptoir brick-and-mortar (it had been a pop-up to that point) and I was going to be his sous chef. We were closed for two months in preparation for the opening and while we were closed, Guerrilla Tacos started taking off. At some point, Gary called me and asked if I was ready to come back to work and I told him, I think it'd be better for me to really give this a go.

I remember the day Jonathan Gold showed up at the cart. Of course I knew him from working in restaurants. He had reviewed every restaurant that I worked at except L'Auberge. *Holy shit, that's Jonathan Gold, at my taco cart.* We had a radio on, playing the Dodgers game. We talked a little shit about the Dodgers and how they always choke in the playoffs, and always to teams that wear red—the Cardinals, the Phillies, the Reds, whatever. *Holy shit, I'm talking about the Dodgers with Jonathan Gold.*

For people who may not be from L.A. or know who Jonathan is, it's hard to overstate his influence here. You get busy when the J Gold reviews you. Very busy. It's like zero to one hundred overnight. I'd watched it happen in the restaurants I'd worked in over the years and to my friends' places.

"I'll have a lamb," he said.

Fuck. We were out of the lamb. It was a braised lamb shank with beef tongue, zucchini roasted on the plancha with garlic, fresh cherry tomatoes, and chile de árbol. We had been tweeting it and Instagramming it all day. But I had literally just served the last portion of lamb to somebody the moment before he ordered it. If I could have I would have taken that lamb taco out of that other customer's hands and given it to Jonathan. I would have. He was cool about it though and he ordered some other things. And then, of course, he jokingly mentioned that we run out of things in his review, after he'd come back to the cart maybe eight or nine times.

The other part about getting a review from Jonathan is you get people coming to you who expect great things. They expect you to make something that's going to change their lives. It's a double-edged sword in a way. You're exposed to more people. Then people expect something that you can't give them. It's very stressful. Especially when you're selling tacos that cost $4, $5, $8—rather than $1.25 at the taco truck around the corner. But my tacos have the best ingredients in them. Foie gras. The same Santa Barbara sea urchin they serve at Nobu. Butter that costs $19 a pound.

And as much as I was living my dream, it was still stressful work. Everything was me in those early days. I'd go to the farmers' market by myself and spend Tuesday nights prepping, braising things, and reducing sauces in the kitchen in my apartment, covering the blender with towels so it wouldn't wake up my neighbors at 3 a.m. Then I'd wake up early in the morning and make the fresh salsas, put the meats and produce into an ice chest, load everything up in the car, hit up this guy in El Sereno who sold me fresh eggs from the chickens in his backyard, drive it all down to the Art District, unload, set up the cart, fill the chafing dish with water, hang up the lights, and then start service.

It was fucking exhausting. But the real challenges were yet to come.

The first time we got shut down by the police was in front of Café Dulce. Some beat cops came up and asked for my permit. I said I forgot it at home. Of course, you can't even get a permit to make tacos on a cart on the street in L.A. It's always going to be illegal. Obviously the cops knew that as well as I did. "Pack it up," they said. I asked who called it in and they motioned to the Starbucks across the street. We never went back to Dulce after that.

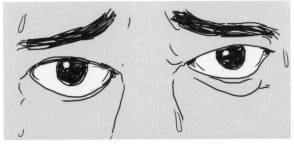

In all, we were shut down three times in that first year. That's why Tanya suggested our name—Guerrilla Tacos—because it was like guerrilla warfare. Where were we going to be next? Would we be shut down? It felt like a game, and not always a fun game.

The second time was at a private event. The worst was when it happened in the Arts District, on our home turf, in front of Handsome, at our normal Wednesday service.

The cops showed up right before our big rush, once again asking for our permit. I showed the cops my little sanitation bucket and a little serve-safe certificate I'd posted at the cart. They just kind of rolled their eyes. They wouldn't even let me give the tacos away to our regulars. I was handing people what I'd made and they were putting $10, $20 bills into the tip jar. The cops pushed everybody away, and all this food was wasted.

That one felt like a smack in the face because it must have come from somebody in the area. Cops don't just show up to shut down taco venders on the street in L.A.—at 5 p.m. no less. They come only if they're called there. So it felt for the first time like maybe we weren't totally accepted.

What's worse is, Tanya and I had planned a vacation to Chicago for our six-year wedding anniversary and to see the Dodgers play the Cubs at Wrigley Field. And the one-year anniversary of Guerrilla Tacos was coming up later that month. We had our regular service scheduled at Handsome for the next week. I had one week. And I knew Guerrilla Tacos had to evolve.

But how?

While we were in Chicago, between attending Dodgers games and curling up in the fetal position in my hotel from the pain of having contracted shingles from stress, I was making calls to find a food truck. I knew we had to become more legit. Not fully legit, just semi-legit. I needed to give the cops a reason not to shut us down. And the food truck is as essential to street food as the brown paper bag is to booze—it's a way to hide in plain sight.

I didn't want people to think less of us because we went from the cart to the truck. By 2013, trucks were already on their way out. It seemed at the time that a lot of the trucks were just gimmicky in concept. Oftentimes they were very specific to one item, one type of preparation or exotic eye-catching cuisine. The cart had cred, but it had proved to be a liability. And I'd been wary of getting a food truck because I knew it could take a long time. It took my friend Ricky from Ricky's Fish Tacos four months to get his truck.

I lucked out because after making five or six different calls I was referred to somebody who owned this food truck in Sun Valley. We were back in L.A. on a Monday, and on Tuesday, we met with this guy Harry. By Wednesday, we had a lease agreement. We signed on Thursday. Boom!

But I quickly learned that getting a food truck is not as easy as just finding a vehicle. First you pay a $4,000 deposit. Which I borrowed. Then you have to get a business permit, seller's permit, workers' comp, truck insurance, serve-safe certificate. Basically it means opening a restaurant on wheels. We had to do that in two days. I cleared my savings account, borrowed the rest, and ran around town like a madman all Tuesday getting that together.

Somehow I made it, and we had normal service at Handsome from 5 p.m. to 9 p.m. on Wednesday. I'm proud to say that we didn't skip a beat. We pulled in at our scheduled time and our regulars were surprised to see us. We had been shut down one week before that.

When I went and picked up the truck early that morning, I was pretty daunted. When I walked inside of it my first thought was, it's fucking huge, there's so much space. It's too big! But all of a sudden I had a deep-fryer, I had more space so I could do some more inventive things. I could store things. I could have several things on the stove top and some on the plancha.

Driving around in the truck was like driving a tank. Things were getting tossed around, there were clinks and clangs and squeaks and grinding noises. Driving that thing was a nightmare.

Before I'd gotten shut down, *Eater* had never written anything about us. This was in the more tabloid days of *Eater.* But when we got shut down, they called me right away. And when that story dropped, once people got wind of it, that combined with the new-found mobility of the truck, created a new model for Guerrilla Tacos. We were doing more covers and parking at cafes, not just in the Arts District but all over town—from Mid-City to Venice. We started doing Thursday nights in front of Silver Lake Wine, where you could take your tacos inside and get a wine pairing along with them. Now all of a sudden we could hire staff to work the truck to make that all happen. We also had to make more money to pay for the truck and the employees.

Running a food truck is the hardest thing I've ever done. I was running a kitchen so I had the same worries as at other restaurants—no-show employees, leaky roof, running out of gas. But added onto that was no parking, breaking down on the freeway, flat tires, stopping for gas, getting into a fender bender, stuck in traffic.

The first two months were the hardest. And the truck started to change how we did our food.

When we were on the cart, I was doing crazy stuff. Pozole. Crazy. I was making that at home and packing it out for service. I look at old menus and . . . what was I thinking? I did a coconut shrimp taco with sweet habanero jelly. That was very labor-intensive. I had to clean the shrimp, butterfly them, batter them, and deep-fry them. And I didn't have a deep-fryer. I was doing blood and chocolate clams. Veal sweetbreads. We were doing tamales customers could order to-go for the holidays.

We had to pare down a little once we got on the truck. I had to settle down a little bit. People expect you to be on time and be consistent about your food. And it wasn't just me cooking, and I couldn't stay up all night doing it at home. I was still limited with a truck—there's nowhere to braise anything, there's nowhere to pressure-cook things, there's nowhere to plug things in easily.

I know the moment we got the truck is the moment we really became Guerrilla Tacos. But you never feel settled on a truck. I still don't feel settled. The truck is kind of a metaphor for what we are doing with the food. We have to keep moving around, changing course, we're always avoiding catastrophe, and we have to be nimble and figure out what's best for every situation.

Perhaps my finest moment on the truck was the very week we opened back up. The cops who had shut us down the week prior came and visited us. They saw my "A" health code sign and smiled at me. I stuck my head out of the window and I said, "Can I get you gentlemen anything to eat?" and they ordered a couple of tacos.

CHICKEN TACO

This is the first taco I made that first day I set up the cart on the street in August 2012. There's nothing too special about this combination—the marinade is pretty classic (but I don't use bell pepper the way many do), and the method is quite typical. The turmeric is key—it adds that great orange color and also does a lot to help break down the chicken meat. There's no BS like seared cauliflower, uni, slow-cooked meats, etc. You can get that kind of thing everywhere else in this book. This is just a good grilled chicken taco, done well. But don't fuck it up. Marinate the chicken overnight. Grill on a hibachi or something similar with good mesquite coals.

Mostly, this is about making the marinade ahead of time and grilling the chicken to get that smoky, slightly caramelized taste and roasted-to-moist texture. It's best to prep and marinate the night before you cook dinner, but the morning of the day you're going to eat works, too.

Marinade

½ cup fresh lemon juice

½ cup fresh lime juice

½ cup fresh orange juice

1 tablespoon kosher salt

1 teaspoon cracked black pepper

1 teaspoon powdered turmeric

1 teaspoon garlic powder

1 teaspoon onion powder

3 pounds boneless skinless chicken thighs

Raw Tomatillo Salsa

1 pound tomatillos (preferably tomatillos milperos, the small purple-colored ones about the size of a quarter), husked and rinsed

1 avocado, pitted and peeled

2 serrano chiles, stemmed

To make the marinade: In a large baking dish, combine the lemon juice, lime juice, orange juice, salt, pepper, turmeric, garlic powder, and onion powder.

Add the chicken to the marinade, turn to coat evenly, and refrigerate for at least 2 hours or up to 24 hours. Remove from the fridge and allow to sit at room temperature for about 30 minutes before grilling.

To make the raw tomatillo salsa: Meanwhile, in a food processor, combine the tomatillos, avocado, serranos, garlic, and cilantro and season with salt. Juice the limes on top. Cover and pulse three or four times—pop, pop, pop—then let it blend a while. You'll start to see the seeds. Keep it chunky though. Taste it and season with more salt.

Prepare a hot fire in a charcoal grill or heat a gas grill to medium-high.

Shake the marinade off the chicken and then place the meat on the grill. Let cook for 20 to 25 minutes, turning and moving it in and out of the direct heat until it's a nice color. Take the chicken off the

fire, cover it with aluminum foil. Let it rest for 3 minutes, then chop into 1-inch pieces.

Layer the chicken, salsa, onion, and cilantro on the tortillas. Serve immediately.

6 garlic cloves

1 bunch of cilantro

Kosher salt

4 to 6 limes

½ red onion, sliced very thin

1 cup chopped cilantro, stems and leaves

12 corn tortillas, warmed (see page 29)

PORK SPARERIB TACO

The idea for these sparerib tacos came from my Tia Hermelinda. She'd make these spareribs for my Uncle Chuckie Boy when he'd come home from his roofing job. I remember I once went with him to go get money from loan sharks. He was a real hustler and businessman. Uncle Chuckie is still around. He has a flattop and he wears a ton of gold, like, more than a rapper.

You have to really cook the cartilage in the meat until it's soft and beautiful.

3 leeks

2 racks pork spareribs (about 4 pounds total)

7 carrots, peeled and rough chopped

2 yellow onions, peeled and diced into 1-inch pieces

2 stalks celery, diced into 1-inch pieces

1 head of garlic, pierced with a knife

1 bunch of flat-leaf parsley, stems and all

6 bay leaves

8 thyme sprigs

12 peppercorns

2 whole cloves

1 star anise

Two 750-ml bottles dry white wine

Preheat the oven to 325°F.

Remove the green parts and roots from the leeks. Cut the whites into large dice. Give them a cold water bath to remove all the dirt, then remove from the water and drain.

In a large roasting pan, combine the spareribs, leeks, carrots, onions, celery, garlic, parsley, bay leaves, thyme, peppercorns, cloves, and star anise. Pour in the wine and enough water to just about cover the ribs. Cover the dish with oven-safe plastic wrap and aluminum foil. Place the roasting pan over two burners on high heat and cook until the foil starts to rise with steam. Place in the oven and bake for 8 hours.

To make the carrot-habanero salsa: In a 12-inch cast-iron skillet over medium-high heat, warm the olive oil. Add the onion and sauté until translucent, about 3 minutes. Then, add the carrot and cook for 4 minutes, or until soft. Add the bell pepper and sauté for 3 minutes. Add the habanero and cook for 1 minute. Add the garlic and cook for 2 minutes. Remove from the heat and season with salt. Slide all the ingredients into a food processor and puree. When smooth, mix in the lime juice. Set aside.

In a bowl, combine the sliced onion, oregano, mint leaves, and 1½ teaspoons salt and stir until mixed. Set aside until you're ready to garnish.

Remove the pan from the oven, uncover, and let cool. Remove the spareribs and discard the rest. The cartilage should be soft enough to cut. If it's tough, you didn't cook it long enough and it should go back into the oven for an hour before checking again. Dice up the meat with a butcher's knife and season heavily with salt. In a pan over medium-high heat, sauté the pork until crispy.

Layer sparerib meat and salsa on the tortillas and garnish with the marinated onions. Serve immediately.

Carrot-Habanero Salsa

1 tablespoon extra-virgin olive oil

¼ cup chopped white onion

1 cup peeled, very thinly sliced carrot coins

1 yellow bell pepper, seeded and sliced into thin strips

1 habanero chile, stemmed

2 garlic cloves, peeled and chopped

Kosher salt

2 tablespoons fresh lime juice

2 cups thinly sliced white onion

2 tablespoons dried oregano

1 cup fresh mint leaves, torn from stems

Kosher salt

16 corn tortillas, warmed (see page 29)

PERRON-STYLE TACO

This taco is reminiscent of my travels down to Baja California and eating at food stands in the suburbs of Rosarito, at a place called Tacos el Gerente. I've also seen a version of this taco in Mexicali, so I think it's more of a northern-style taco. You're using skirt steak, which can be a little tough, so I recommend cooking it to medium instead of medium-rare. Try to remember to breathe while you're eating because this is a super-addictive taco. *Perron* translates to "bitchin' " I think—it's just a bitchin' taco.

To make the backyard marinade: In a large bowl, mix together the vegetable oil, cumin, chili powder, garlic powder, onion powder, black pepper, onions, oranges, and vinegar and season with salt.

Add the steak to the marinade, turn to evenly coat, and leave in the refrigerator to marinate overnight.

Rinse the pinto beans and remove any imperfect ones or small stones. Put the beans in a pot, cover with water, and set over medium heat until they're bubbling. Add the onion, bay leaves, and garlic and simmer slowly. Don't salt your beans until they're done; otherwise it will extract the water from the beans and you want them to absorb the water. When the beans are cooked and break apart when pressed with a spoon, remove from the heat and season with salt. Set aside to steep.

Prepare a medium charcoal or mesquite fire in a grill or heat a gas grill to 525°F.

Remove the meat from the marinade and discard the marinade. Grill the meat for about 6 minutes, or until cooked to medium, turning once or twice. If using a gas grill, grill for 3 to 4 minutes with the lid on. Alternatively, in a 12-inch cast-iron skillet over high heat, warm the vegetable oil. Add the meat and cook for about 5 minutes, turning once. Once cooked, set aside in a container covered with foil to let it rest for 5 minutes, then chop into 1½-inch pieces.

continued

Backyard Marinade

1 cup vegetable oil

1 tablespoon ground cumin

1 tablespoon light chili powder

2 tablespoons garlic powder

2 tablespoons onion powder

1 tablespoon freshly ground black pepper

2 white onions, thinly sliced

2 oranges, thinly sliced into rings (do not peel)

¼ cup white vinegar

Kosher salt

3 pounds skirt steak, sliced into 3-by-5-inch pieces, ½ inch thick, like fajitas

2 cups dried pinto beans

1 yellow onion, quartered

2 bay leaves

1 head of garlic, halved lengthwise

Kosher salt

1 tablespoon extra-virgin olive oil (optional)

Seasoned Jalapeños

6 jalapeño chiles

Kosher salt

3 limes, halved

1 pound Monterey Jack cheese, cut into 2- to 3-inch slices

Twelve 5-inch flour tortillas, warmed (see page 29)

Pico de Gallo Salsa (page 42) for topping

Mexican-Style Guacamole (page 58) for topping

To make the seasoned jalapeños: On the high-heat grill or in a 6-inch cast-iron skillet over high heat, roast the jalapeños and get them nice and charred, about 4 minutes. Once they're roasted, cut off the stems, and slice the chiles. Season liberally with salt and squeeze the limes over the top. Set aside.

In a pan over medium heat, add about 1⅓ ounces cheese to each warmed tortilla, and melt the cheese so it's kind of quesadilla-ish. Once it's melted, put the tortillas on a plate. Add the meat and beans, top with pico de gallo and guacamole, and garnish with the seasoned jalapeños. Serve immediately.

BEEF TENDON TACO

Whenever I get home from a trip, one of my favorite things to eat is pho. My favorite part of the soup is the tendon. I figured why not make a taco with tendon? Tendon being so tough, it needs to be braised for a very long time. It's got a chew to it that necessitates frying the tortilla. For this version I cook the tendon, stuff the tortilla, and then deep fry it all to result in a crispy outside texture with the gooey, wonderful tendon on the inside.

To make the saigon slaw: In a mixing bowl, combine the carrots, cucumbers, bean sprouts, cabbage, red pepper flakes, peanuts, cilantro, and mint and stir to mix. Pour the salsa liberally over mixture. Toss, toss, toss it together, and taste. It should be spicy, salty, umami goodness. Refrigerate until ready to serve.

To make the raw habanero salsa: In a food processor, combine the habaneros, garlic, salt, and lime juice and puree on high speed for about 1 minute, or until thoroughly blended. Set aside.

Preheat the oven to 325°F.

Put the beef tendons in a roasting pan and cover about three-fourths of the way with water. Add the onion and season liberally with salt and pepper. Cover with oven-safe plastic wrap and two layers of aluminum foil. Roast for about 8 hours; at this point the tendon should look like a thick, translucent jelly. Drain and discard the liquid.

Cut the tendons into about 3-inch pieces. Place two tendon pieces inside each tortilla and fold in half. Make sure the tendon is fully tucked inside the tortillas because it'll stick to the fryer. You can use toothpicks to keep the tortillas closed while frying.

In a 10-inch cast-iron skillet, heat the vegetable oil to 365°F. Add the tortillas in batches and fry until golden brown, about 3 minutes. Remove from the skillet, drain excess oil, and keep warm.

Put two tacos on each plate. Top with habanero salsa and an abundant amount of slaw. Serve immediately.

Saigon Slaw

4 carrots, peeled and julienned

2 cucumbers, peeled, seeded, and julienned

1 cup bean sprouts

6 cups shredded red cabbage

2 tablespoons dried red pepper flakes

1 cup roasted salted peanuts, crushed

2 cups fresh cilantro leaves

1 cup fresh mint leaves

1 recipe Salsa Bruja (page 45)

Raw Habanero Salsa

8 habanero chiles, stemmed

2 garlic cloves, peeled

1 tablespoon kosher salt

1 cup fresh lime juice

2 pounds beef tendons (order it through your butcher)

1 yellow onion, peeled and halved

Kosher salt

Freshly ground black pepper

Twelve 6-inch corn tortillas, warmed (see page 29)

2 cups vegetable oil

MUSHROOM AND FIDEO TACO

This taco is inspired by the tacos de fideo from Mexico, and a childhood memory. When I was a kid, we used to take leftover spaghetti that my mom would make, warm up a couple tortillas, and enjoy it as an after-school snack. In this recipe, I like to showcase wild mushrooms while staying true to the comfort of having the tacos be a little bit rich and satisfying the way they were when I was young. These tacos do not need any herbs. This is a very home-style taco with really nice ingredients. It should be straightforward, and what you want to taste is the pasta and the cheese. Wild mushrooms are best for this. But you have to clean them very, very well.

¼ cup lard

4 cups broken angel hair pasta (roughly 2-inch pieces)

Kosher salt

1 pound wild mushrooms, such as morels or chanterelles (see Note, opposite)

3 tablespoons unsalted butter

2 garlic cloves, pierced with a knife

4 thyme sprigs

1½ cups grated Parmesan cheese, or as desired

2 tablespoons cracked black pepper

12 corn tortillas, warmed (see page 29)

Salsa Casera (page 80) for garnishing

Chopped chives for garnishing

In a 12-inch cast-iron skillet over medium-high heat, melt the lard. Add the pasta and brown for about 4 minutes, turning occasionally. This is a home-style way of cooking pasta that I haven't really seen anyone else do outside of Mexican families. Not all of the noodles will be browned as much as the others but that's okay.

While you're browning the pasta, in a large pot over high heat, bring 3 quarts water to a boil. Add about 3 tablespoons salt, then add the browned pasta and cook for 6 to 7 minutes, until al dente.

Meanwhile, fill the sink with 6 inches of cold water. Add the mushrooms and push them around, rubbing off the dirt and impurities with your fingers. The dirt should sink to the bottom, the mushrooms should bob to the top. Pick up the mushrooms with your hands, drain and clean the sink, and then rinse the mushrooms one more time under running water. Repeat this process a second time. Set the mushrooms on a wire rack. Depending on the size of the mushroom, cut in half or quarters. You want the pieces to be 2 to 3 inches in size because they will shrink as you cook.

In the same pan you used to cooked your noodles, over medium heat, combine the butter and garlic and cook until the garlic is aromatic, about 30 seconds. Add the mushrooms. Cook for about 5 minutes, add the thyme, cook for 30 seconds more, and then turn off the heat.

Drain the pasta, reserving about ¼ cup of pasta water to help cook it the rest of the way and incorporate the cheese.

Remove the thyme from the mushrooms and add the pasta and reserved pasta water. Turn the heat to medium-high and add the cheese. Mix thoroughly and add the black pepper. Cook for about 1½ minutes, until it's a thick mixture of pasta with mushrooms. If it's too liquidy, just cook longer. Season with salt, and if you want to add more cheese, add more cheese.

Divide the pasta mixture among the tortillas and garnish with a little bit of the salsa casera. Serve immediately.

NOTE If you can't find wild mushrooms, button mushrooms will work.

SHISHITO PEPPER TACO with Poached Egg

I first had shishito peppers while eating sushi at Tokyo Kitchen in Montclair. After having them there, simply sautéed with a little furikake, I fell in love with them. So I try to use some of my favorite mild peppers to play off the fattiness from the poached egg.

To make the tomato-pepita salsa: In a 10-inch cast-iron skillet over medium heat, warm 1 tablespoon of the vegetable oil. Add the pepitas and guajillos and toast until aromatic, about 2 minutes. Remove from the heat and set aside.

Add the remaining 1 tablespoon oil to the skillet. Add the onion and garlic and sauté over medium heat until the onion turns translucent, about 3 minutes. Add the tomatoes, water, and pepitas. Cover and cook until the tomatoes are soft, about 12 minutes. Season with salt.

Transfer the contents of the skillet to a blender and blend on high speed until completely smooth. Add the vinegar and adjust to taste.

To make the dashi: Put the kombu in a bowl, cover with cold water, and allow to bloom for 10 minutes. Remove the kombu and put it in a 2-quart saucepan with the scallions, bonito flakes, and water. Bring to a simmer over medium heat and cook for 8 minutes. Remove from the heat and allow to steep for about 20 minutes. Then strain and discard the solids. Set aside.

In a large bowl, combine ⅓ cup dashi, the white soy sauce, and ⅓ cup rice vinegar and stir. Add the yuzu juice, to add more or less acid, to make a ponzu sauce. Set aside.

Fill a small (2-quart) saucepan with water halfway up to the top. Bring it to a simmer over medium heat. Add the 1 teaspoon rice vinegar and a pinch of salt. One at a time, carefully crack each eggshell on a flat surface and add the eggs to the water. Cook

continued

Tomato-Pepita Salsa

2 tablespoons vegetable oil

2 tablespoons pepitas (pumpkin seeds)

3 guajillo chiles, stemmed and seeded

½ red onion, rough chopped

4 garlic cloves, peeled and halved

5 Roma tomatoes, cored and halved

1 cup water

Kosher salt

3 tablespoons cider vinegar, or to taste

Dashi

One 4-by-2-inch piece kombu

6 scallions (white parts only)

1 cup loosely packed bonito flakes

1 cup water

⅓ cup white soy sauce (also called shiro)

⅓ cup rice vinegar, plus 1 teaspoon

Yuzu juice to taste (or 1 part tangerine juice to 1 part lemon juice)

Kosher salt

6 eggs

Freshly cracked black pepper

1 pound shishito peppers, stemmed

1 tablespoon vegetable oil

2 Roma tomatoes, sliced

8 corn tortillas, warmed (see page 29)

2 tablespoons furikake

2 tablespoons extra-virgin olive oil, preferably Spanish (optional)

for about 30 seconds, turning in the water gently without breaking the yolks. Use a slotted spoon to transfer the eggs to a paper towel or napkin. Immediately season with salt and black pepper.

Wash and thoroughly dry the shishitos and place in a bowl. Drizzle with the vegetable oil and season liberally with salt.

Prepare a hot fire in a charcoal grill, heat a gas grill to high, or place a cast-iron skillet over high heat. Add the shishitos and roast until they are blistered and puffy in places and turn a deeper green all over.

In a bowl, gently toss together the shishitos and ponzu sauce until fully coated.

Layer the shishitos, eggs, tomato slices, and salsa on the tortillas. Sprinkle with the furikake and drizzle with some olive oil, if you have it. Serve immediately.

PIG HEAD TACO with Lentils and Fried Quail Egg

This is a weekend project for a dinner party. Basically you're making head cheese. My inspiration comes from a dish Walter made at L'Auberge with duck confit, a little disc of head cheese, and a fried egg on a base of lightly dressed frisée.

Pig feet are hard to debone, but they're also the best and most flavorful option because they have bones. Pig ears are good because they're boneless and therefore easier to work with, cut into pieces, and mix with the pork shoulder.

Preheat the oven to 325°F.

Season the pork shoulder liberally with salt and pepper. Wrap in oven-safe plastic wrap.

In a large roasting pan with 4-inch sides, combine the seasoned pork, pig head or ears and feet, white onion, celery, half of the carrots, and the peppercorns. Add the white wine and enough cold water to completely submerge the pork. Cover tightly with foil. Crank the heat to high for 10 minutes, or until the foil starts to balloon from the steam. Put the pan in the oven and forget about it for 8 hours. (If you can't fit everything into one pan, use a separate pot for the pork shoulder and divide the other ingredients proportionately.)

In a 4-quart saucepan over medium-high heat, melt 1 tablespoon of the butter. Add the bacon and cook for 4 minutes. Add the yellow onion, garlic, and remaining carrots and cook for 5 minutes. Add the lentils and cook for another 1 minute. Add the tomato paste and gently sauté for 2 minutes. Add the veal stock, red wine, and port and turn the heat to high. When the liquid starts to boil, light the surface of the pan with a long lighter (the kind you'd use to light a grill) and flambé the alcohol. Turn the heat to medium-low and add the rosemary, bay leaves, and orange zest and cook for 1½ hours, (Cook the lentils until they're "to the tooth" as we say—cooked but still sturdy.) Strain the liquid into a saucepan and reduce it by half. Pick out and discard the rosemary and orange zest, if necessary. Return the stock to the lentils and cook it down until it assumes the texture of a thin chili. Season with salt and pepper. Set aside.

continued

One 2-pound bone-in pork shoulder

Kosher salt

Freshly ground black pepper

1 pig head or 8 pig ears and 4 pig feet (about 3 pounds including bones)

1 white onion, diced into large pieces

4 celery stalks, tops removed, diced into large pieces

5 carrots, peeled and diced into large pieces

12 black peppercorns

One 750-ml bottle dry white wine

4 tablespoons unsalted butter

4 ounces bacon end pieces (preferably Nueske's or some very smoky bacon) or ham hock

1 yellow onion, cut into large pieces

1 head of garlic, stabbed with a knife to allow the flavor to release

1 cups green lentils (preferably Le Puy)

3 tablespoons tomato paste

1 cup veal or chicken stock

Remove the meat from the oven—the head or feet, should be fall-off-the-bone tender; ears should be very, very tender to the bite—and allow to cool. Shred the meat off the bone of the shoulder and the feet; if using ears, slice the meat into thin slices, lengthwise. If you have a head, put it in a roasting pan and let it cool a bit—but not too much; you don't want the collagen to get too cool and sticky. When it's still warm, working with your hands with gloves on, pull all the meat away from the bones. Season with salt, pepper, and the vinegar.

Unspool some plastic wrap onto a countertop. Working in batches, line up all the meat across the plastic. You want to end up with tightly packed rolls of pork about 3½ inches in diameter and about 10 inches long. Roll the plastic wrap around the meat and move it back and forth to compact into a log. If any log is not about 3½ inches in diameter, add or remove as much meat as is necessary to get the proportion right. It should end up with the texture of head cheese or a rustic paté. When you have your rolls, close off the ends with plastic and put them in the freezer to chill.

Line a baking sheet with wax paper. Line a large dish with paper towels. Place the all-purpose flour on a large plate. Add the eggs to a large bowl. Put the panko on another large plate. Set them next to the stove.

When the pork is chilled, with the plastic wrap still on, cut into 1½-inch slices, and then remove the plastic. Next, dip the pork in the flour, then in the eggs, then in the panko and place on the prepared baking sheet.

In an 8-inch sauté pan over medium-high heat, warm the vegetable oil. Add the pork pieces four at a time; they should start sizzling at once. Try to cover the pork with oil, or flip once the bottoms are golden. Remove from the oil and place on the prepared dish to drain.

In a pot over medium-low heat, warm the lentils.

In a nonstick pan over medium-low heat, melt 1 tablespoon butter. Add 5 quail eggs and fry until the yolks are a little runny, and then transfer to a plate. Repeat with the remaining butter and eggs.

Top each tortilla with a spoonful of lentils, one pig disk, and a fried quail egg and garnish with salsa. Serve immediately.

3 cups dry red wine

1 cup port wine

1 rosemary sprig

2 bay leaves

Zest of 1 orange

¼ cup white vinegar

3 cups unbleached all-purpose flour

8 eggs, beaten

4 cups panko, finely ground in the food processor

¼ cup vegetable oil

15 quail eggs

15 corn tortillas, warmed (see page 29)

Arbol Salsa (page 34) for garnishing

GRILLED SHRIMP TACO

Use Gulf shrimp if you can find them. We use 16/20-size shrimp—the numbers are the number of shrimp that it takes to make up 1 pound. I like the combination of the sweetness of the shrimp and the sweetness of the Thai peanut curry. This is kind of my take on a chicken satay.

Curry

1 tablespoon vegetable oil

1 tablespoon Thai red curry paste

1 teaspoon powdered turmeric

1¼ cups canned coconut milk

2 tablespoons peanut butter

1 tablespoon sugar

2 tablespoons fish sauce, or to taste

Kosher salt

2 pounds (16/20 size) shrimp, shells included

½ cup vegetable oil

1 tablespoon onion powder

1 tablespoon garlic powder

1 teaspoon dried parsley

2 tablespoons finely minced garlic

1½ teaspoons kosher salt

Thai Slaw

2 cups peeled and julienned carrots

1 cup peeled and julienned cucumbers

¼ cup toasted cashews, crushed

½ cup chopped fresh cilantro, chopped, including up to 2 inches of stem below the last leaf branch

To make the curry: In a 12-inch cast-iron skillet over medium heat, warm the vegetable oil. Add the curry paste and turmeric and lightly sauté until they become aromatic and incorporated, about 1 minute. Whisk in the coconut milk until it starts to bubble and the curry paste dissolves. Add the peanut butter and sugar and continue to whisk for 4 minutes, until it turns bright yellow. Turn off the heat and season with fish sauce and salt. Set aside.

Prepare a hot fire in a charcoal grill or heat a gas grill to high.

Using a paring knife, cut from the top of the shrimp to the bottom of the tail. Make a small incision to the point where it's almost cut through, slowly move the knife down to the bottom, and open it up like a book. Repeat for all the shrimp.

In a bowl, mix together the vegetable oil, onion powder, garlic powder, parsley, minced garlic, and salt. Add the shrimp and toss to coat evenly. Skewer the shrimp, about four shrimp per skewer, shells all facing in the same direction.

Grill the shrimp, shell-side down, over the hot coals, until they're 90 percent done, about 1½ minutes per side. They should be nicely charred. If you get flare-ups, cover the grill to manage the flame. Set aside and cover to keep warm.

To make the thai slaw: In a bowl, toss together the carrots, cucumbers, cashews, cilantro, mint, lime juice, and serranos until mixed. Season with salt.

Shell the shrimp and divide among the tortillas. Top with the curry, then the slaw. Add some lemon juice and finish with olive oil. Serve immediately.

½ cup whole fresh mint leaves, torn from stem

Juice of 4 limes

4 serrano chiles, stemmed and sliced very thin

Kosher salt

10 corn tortillas, warmed (see page 29)

Juice of 2 lemons

2 tablespoons extra-virgin olive oil, preferably Spanish

CALAMARI TACO

You know those beach towns in Baja, like Puerto Nuevo or Rosarito Beach, where there's always a guy in the street walking around trying to get you into their restaurant to eat lobster? Rooftop dining, ocean view, and something like $15 for a huge meal—chips and salsa, guacamole, calamari steak, tortilla soup, and then the lobster. Wash it down with margaritas and cold beer. It's touristy as hell, but I love it. At this one place, La Teraza in Puerto Nuevo, they serve cubed calamari steak with garlic on plastic spears. I probably had this for the first time as a kid with my dad, but Tanya and I still sneak down to Baja for a couple days whenever we have the time, and usually have this type of meal at least once.

Loroco is used a lot in South American cooking. It's a vine that grows buds with an herby little bite to them. I like to pickle them, and I think it adds a lot to a dish. The salsa gives a little kick—actually, a lot of kick—along with the complexity of the spices in the pickle, and the blistered tomatoes get a little sweet and sticky, and provide varied texture. If you don't like heat, you won't like this salsa!! It is two parts serrano to one part habanero. Wear gloves to make this one. It should be chunky but spreadable on a spoon. Pair the tacos with cold beer.

To make the habanero-serrano-tomatillo salsa: Over a fire on an outdoor grill, in a basket, on the stove top, or with a Searzall or blow torch—however it is easiest for you to get the chiles fully blackened—roast your serranos and habaneros. I don't stem them because this way I can still handle them if needed, and the heat stays somewhat sealed inside (but be careful!). Just make sure they get blackened all over but are not ashy and then pull them off the heat.

Remove the stems and throw the chiles in a food processor with the tomatillos. You want this salsa kind of chunky, not as smooth as other salsas. Just *pop pop pop* in the food processor and then run it a bit. It's rustic. Add the vinegar (for a little sourness, but also to add some liquid) and garlic, season with salt, and let the processor run for a while longer. Set aside.

continued

Roasted Habanero-Serrano-Tomatillo Salsa

4 serrano chiles

2 habanero chiles

1 cup tomatillos, husked and rinsed

¼ cup white vinegar

4 garlic cloves, peeled

Kosher salt

Pickled Loroco

1½ cups water

1 cup white vinegar

½ cup sugar

1 tablespoon mustard seeds

1 dried chile de árbol, stemmed;
1 teaspoon coriander seeds;
3 allspice berries; 1 bay leaf;
1 cinnamon stick; and/or
1 star anise

8 ounces fresh loroco, buds only,
washed

½ teaspoon onion powder

½ teaspoon garlic powder

½ teaspoon Old Bay seasoning

½ teaspoon dried parsley

6 calamari steaks

Kosher salt

Freshly ground black pepper

4 tablespoons unsalted butter

4 garlic cloves, peeled and
finely minced

2 tablespoons vegetable oil

1 cup cherry tomatoes, halved

1 thyme sprig (optional)

6 corn tortillas, warmed
(see page 29)

1 lime, cut into 6 wedges

Purple basil or cilantro for
garnishing

To make the pickled loroco: In a small saucepan over high heat, combine the water, vinegar, and sugar and bring to a boil. Add the mustard seeds and any combination of the chile de árbol, coriander seeds, allspice, bay leaf, cinnamon stick, and star anise. You don't really want to taste any of these in particular; it's more like, What's that other flavor in there?

Put the loroco in a metal bowl or large ceramic container. Once the pickling mixture has come to a boil, immediately pour it over the loroco. Let marinate for about 2 hours, then cover and store in the fridge for up to 2 weeks.

In a small bowl, combine the onion powder, garlic powder, Old Bay seasoning, and dried parsley and stir to mix.

Inspect both sides of the calamari to find the side that has a softer texture. Score this side with little X marks, about ½ inch each. Then flip the steaks and score the skin side all the way across in both directions. Season the steaks with salt and pepper and then dust with the mixed seasonings. You don't want a thick crust, more like an even sprinkle.

In a 12-inch cast-iron skillet over medium-high heat, warm 2 tablespoons of the butter. Once hot, add three of the steaks. Don't crowd the pan. Poke the steaks as they cook—they should have a spring to them, but they shouldn't be tough. You're looking for a texture like a squishy gummy bear. They should get a little color and the spice mixture should be turning golden. Cook for about 1½ minutes on one side and 45 seconds on the flip side. After you turn the steaks, throw in half of the garlic and let it cook for about 1 minute. Remove all the garlic and let the steaks rest. Repeat with the remaining butter, steaks, and garlic.

In a separate pan over high heat, warm the vegetable oil. Add the cherry tomatoes and let them start to blister, then sprinkle with salt. Throw in the thyme, if you have it, and continue to sauté. Once the tomato skins start tearing off, about 5 minutes, turn off the burner.

Cut the calamari into cubes and place on the tortillas in even portions. Squeeze some lime juice over the calamari and add some cherry tomatoes, then the pickled lorocco. Finish it off with the salsa and cilantro. Serve immediately.

AJO BLANCO

While spending time in the south of Spain, we were often served a cold, white soup, called ajo blanco, made with bread, almonds, garlic, water, olive oil, and vinegar. Whenever I taste the components of this soup it always takes me back to Andalucia. This goes very well with all types of shellfish and that's how I like to serve it, or just on its own.

In a food processor, combine the almonds, garlic, olive oil, vinegar, and 1½ tablespoons salt, and process until thoroughly mixed. Add the water and bread and puree until you have a soupy texture. Adjust the seasoning; if it needs a little bit more salt, add salt. If it needs vinegar, add vinegar. Strain through a fine-mesh sieve, discard the solids, and chill in the refrigerator until very cold.

Prepare an ice-water bath in the largest mixing bowl you have by stirring together water and a tray of ice. Set a medium saucepan three-quarters full of water over high heat and bring to a boil.

Using a small paring knife, score a small X at the bottom of each grape. Drop the grapes into the boiling water. After 5 seconds, remove with a slotted spoon and drop into the ice-water bath. When cool, peel off the skins.

Pour the soup into bowls and garnish with apple, grapes, and chives. Serve immediately.

6 ounces blanched Marcona almonds

1 garlic clove, peeled

½ cup extra-virgin olive oil

2 tablespoons sherry vinegar, or to taste

Kosher salt

4 cups water

7 ounces white or sourdough bread

1 cup seedless green grapes

1 green or other tart apple, peeled, cored, and julienned

2 tablespoons minced chives

SQUASH SOUP with Seared Foie Gras and Apples

When working with foie gras, you can either buy whole foie gras lobes or foie gras that is already portioned. I prefer to use Rougie Brand foie gras because it is flash-frozen as soon as it's harvested, which gives you the freshest quality foie you can buy. Order from Rougie online.

1 butternut squash

2 leeks

8 ounces unsalted butter, cubed

2 dried chile moritas

3 thyme sprigs

1 bay leaf

1½ cups sherry wine

4 cups heavy cream

4 cups vegetable stock

Kosher salt

1 pound Grade A foie gras, sliced into 2-ounce pieces

½ cup pepitas (pumpkin seeds)

4 pink lady, Fuji, or any tart firm apples, julienned

Prepare a medium-hot fire in a charcoal grill or heat a gas grill to medium-high.

Put the squash on the grill and roast until the outside is nicely blackened, 30 to 50 minutes, depending on the size, flipping once. (If you don't have a barbecue pit or a grill, you can cut the squash in half, scoop out the seeds, and roast on a baking sheet in a 400°F oven until it's cooked through, about 30 minutes.) Peel the blackened skin off the squash and cut into smaller pieces, about 2-inch cubes. Discard the seeds.

Remove the green parts and root from the leeks. Cut the whites into ½-inch pieces. Give them a cold water bath to remove all the dirt, then remove from the water and drain.

In a large pot or Dutch oven over medium heat, melt the butter. Add the leeks, chile moritas, thyme, and bay leaf and sauté until the leeks are translucent, about 10 minutes. Remove the herbs. Add the cubed squash and sherry and cook until you don't smell alcohol anymore, about 2 minutes. Add the heavy cream and cook for 6 to 8 minutes, stirring often with a wooden spoon to make sure it does not burn. You're just cooking the raw cream flavor out of the soup; make sure to cook the cream well because sometimes people make the mistake of adding heavy cream to soup but not cooking it thoroughly. Add the vegetable stock and cook for about 10 minutes. Remove from the heat.

Transfer the soup to a blender and begin pureeing, carefully, holding the top with a towel (so you don't burn yourself). Season with salt as you go. The consistency of the soup should not be too thick, but it should be able to coat the back of a spoon, almost

the consistency of heavy cream. Return the pureed soup to the pot and keep it over the lowest possible heat until you're ready to serve.

Score the fois gras slices in a crosshatched pattern over one side. In a cast-iron skillet over medium-high heat, sear the foie gras for 1 minute on the scored side and about 30 seconds on the other. (You do not need to add oil because it's pure fat.)

In a small pan over medium-high heat, toast the pepitas until aromatic, about 3 minutes, flipping with a wooden spoon occasionally, so they don't burn.

Ladle the soup into bowls, set the seared foie gras right in middle, and garnish with the apples and pepitas. Serve immediately.

SANTA BARBARA SEA URCHIN SCRAMBLE

This came up because I just had a bunch of leftover sea urchin and some brioche. Make sure the bread is a nice thick cut. You don't want some thin-cut shit. You want it squishy on the inside. I use micro chives to add a little bit of herbaceousness. And then a little bit of heat from the salsa. I guess you could say this is my take on soft scrambled egg with black truffle, a super-classic French dish.

Prepare an ice-water bath in the largest mixing bowl you have by stirring together water and a tray of ice. Cover a plate with paper towels. Set both aside.

Wearing gloves, flip the sea urchin over onto a kitchen towel or a rimmed baking sheet, with the mouth facing up. Take a hard metal spoon in each hand, with the lips facing out—as if you're playing the spoons. Force one spoon into the hole. Tap down on it with the other spoon gingerly until you hear a crack. Then jam them both in and, working the spoons in a pruning-shear motion, crack open the sea urchin. It'll be messy, which is why you have it all laid out on a kitchen towel. Rinse your spoons and carefully scrape the yellow sea urchin roe away from the shell. There should be five portions. Take care not to break up the roe, each portion should come off in a piece, like a small, long tongue (see page 135). Put these pieces into the ice-water bath to clean off any impurities. Set the sea urchin roe on the prepared plate and, using tweezers, remove any more impurities. (You can do this 10 to 20 minutes ahead of time. Pop them in the fridge until you're ready to use.)

In a pan over medium heat, melt 2 tablespoons of the butter. Add the brioche and grill until it's nice and golden brown, flipping as you go and making sure it toasts evenly and doesn't burn.

continued

1 live sea urchin (see Note, page 134)

4 tablespoons unsalted butter

1 piece of thick-cut brioche (about 3 inches thick)

3 eggs

1 tablespoon micro chives, minced

Finishing salt, such as fleur de sel or Maldon sea salt

Roasted Habanero-Serrano Salsa (page 47) for garnishing

In a nonstick pan over medium-low heat, warm the remaining 2 tablespoons butter until it starts to bubble. Crack the eggs into the pan and, using a wooden spoon or silicone whisk, whisk to mix. (You don't want to break down the eggs entirely.) Turn up the heat as you go. Just keep whisking, and pull the eggs off the heat if you have to before they set entirely so that you don't overcook them, about 2 minutes. You want make it almost like a custard. Add the chives and season with salt.

Put the eggs on the bread, the sea urchin on top of the eggs, and garnish with little dollops of salsa around it—you probably don't want too much because you want the buttery sea urchin to stand out. Serve immediately.

WAFFLES

Kids love waffles. I love waffles. Everybody loves waffles. These are my favorite waffles to make for weekend brunch service at the truck. The secret is the malted milk powder.

In a bowl, combine the flour, cornstarch, malted milk powder, baking powder, and salt. Sift onto parchment paper, then put it back into the bowl. In a separate bowl, whisk together the egg, buttermilk, vegetable oil, vanilla, and sugar. Pour your wet ingredients into your dry and whisk it to mix, ten times. Tap the bowl to loosen the batter from the edges. Whisk twice more. You want to keep it a little chunky.

Heat a waffle iron. Once it's hot, pour in the batter and, following the manufacturer's instructions, make golden brown, perfect waffles.

To top the waffles: Add the toppings as you desire—a slab of salted butter, a dusting of powdered sugar, a drizzle of maple syrup, a dollop of mascarpone crema, slices of seasonal fruit. GO CRAZY! Serve immediately.

¾ cup all-purpose flour

¼ cup cornstarch

¼ cup malted milk powder (Carnation brand is fine)

½ teaspoon baking powder

½ teaspoon fine sea salt

1 egg

1 cup buttermilk

⅓ cup vegetable oil

1 teaspoon vanilla extract

1 teaspoon sugar

Choose-Your-Own-Adventure Toppings

Beurre de Barate or other salted, high-fat butter (about 1½ teaspoons per waffle)

Powdered sugar

Real maple syrup

Mascarpone Crema (recipe follows)

Seasonal fruit, such as apples, strawberries, oranges, or bananas, cut and tossed with sugar, then caramelized with a blow torch

MARSCAPONE CREMA

8 ounces mascarpone

2 cups heavy cream

2 tablespoons sugar

Finely grated zest and juice of 1 lemon

In a bowl, whisk together the mascarpone, cream, sugar, and lemon zest and juice until medium-soft peaks form. Store in an airtight container in the refrigerator for up to 4 days.

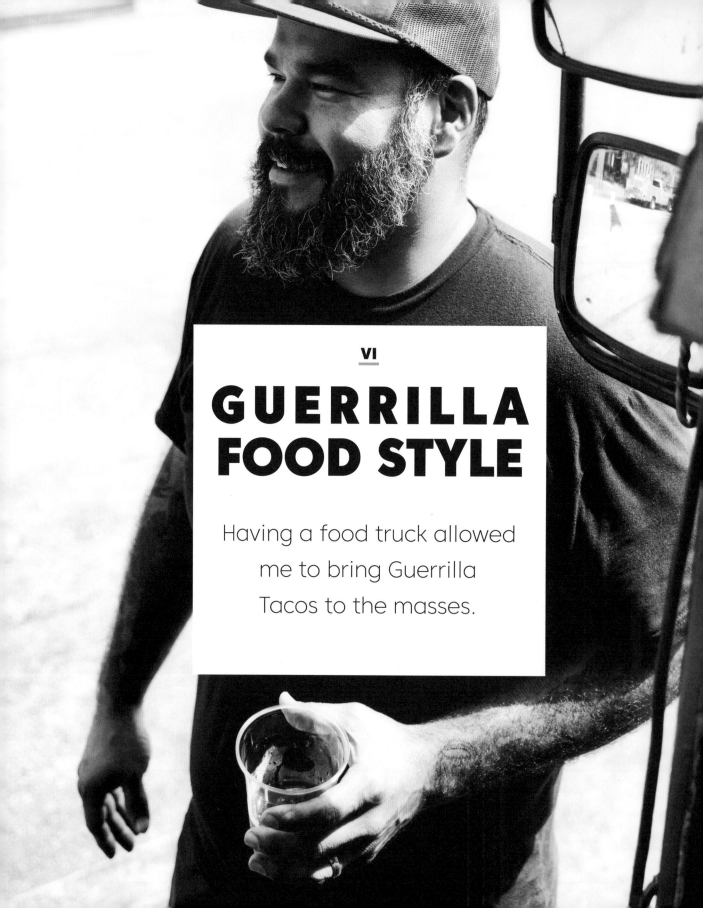

GUERRILLA FOOD STYLE

Having a food truck allowed me to bring Guerrilla Tacos to the masses.

AFTER WE GOT THE FOOD TRUCK, I COULDN'T INTERACT WITH MY CUSTOMERS AS MUCH AS BEFORE. WHEN I STARTED THE CART, I WAS THE FACE OF THE BUSINESS. I'D DEAL WITH ALL THE ISSUES DIRECTLY MYSELF, BUT THEN WITH THE TRUCK THERE WAS NOW THIS BIG WALL BETWEEN ME AND THEM. I MISS THAT PART OF DOING GUERRILLA TACOS, BUT IT ENDED UP BEING A BIT OF A BLESSING IN DISGUISE, BECAUSE THAT'S WHEN I STARTED GETTING DEEPER INTO THE FOOD I WAS MAKING AND REALLY FOUND OUT WHAT MAKES GUERRILLA TACOS *GUERRILLA TACOS*.

When we started the truck, we tried to run it like the cart—just two people working at a time. There was too much room. We weren't using its full capacity. And I was still cooking and prepping at home. We were open only three days a week, the same service as we had for the cart. Then I'd get my monthly lease statement for the truck and be, like, I need to be open more days to make this work. We had to get slightly legit.

I realized I had a deep-fryer at my disposal and that I should be using it. That's when we started doing Baja tacos, hard-shell potato tacos, the pocho taco, and street taters. The menu changed. We had an actual refrigerator. I didn't have to work as much from home, but it took a while to break the habit. I gradually started to figure out how to use the truck to help me build a diverse menu every day without killing myself with extra work to prep for our new service schedule.

When we added extra service days, we still tried to have the attitude of changing the menu every day. It was so fucking hard. I knew people liked it, and I liked doing it, but before, on the cart, it was easier. I could shop at the farmers' market in the morning, go to the fishmonger, maybe stop off at Super King, and have the cart in the back of my Scion all the while. Then I'd roll up to our location and do service, pack up, go home. With the truck I couldn't just pull into some farmers' market and pick up a bunch of micro greens on my way to service. I needed two parking spots and an extra person with me. I needed to start planning.

We started getting complaints that we were always running out of food. Precious ingredients from the farmers' market or the eggs from the guy who keeps chickens in his backyard in El Sereno would run out. We'd be out of a certain dish all of a sudden, in the middle of service at 12 noon. Then we would have to change the menu to do more covers. We made the sweet potato taco standard at some point, and so I had to only think of three to four items each day, versus five, but still it was too much to worry about day in and day out.

I needed somebody outside of my kitchen to tell me that it would be more efficient to do the menu weekly. That was my business partner, Brittney Valles. And that only happened six months before this writing. It's still fresh and we change it every week. That's plenty.

We only ever did service in front of boutique coffee shops in the Arts District (including Handsome Coffee Roasters, Blue Bottle Coffee, and Black Top Coffee) and we always felt like the Arts District was our home.

But then we decided to move around the city more. We had fans who used to come to the Arts District who now lived in Venice. People were asking us to show up in their part of town. I realized we could easily do this, since we have the truck. There was no real reason not to reach more people in more areas of the city. It's all incremental changes with me.

Our visual style developed, too. When we first got the truck, it was just painted blue. We had a little wooden sign that said GUERRILLA TACOS we would hang off the window. That was it.

Alex from L.A. Taco approached me about Red Bull sponsoring us for the painting of the truck by Vyal. I said yes on the condition that we don't have to sell Red Bull. They agreed and Vyal and I got together and I told him our story and he just went crazy, adding his street-art style to our truck. It made us the most recognizable truck in L.A. A big blue truck with graffiti. When we got a new truck, we got Vyal to paint it too. And you can see his work on the cover of this book. Street art is important to our brand. We never saw it as printed or clean lines. We want that L.A. soul in there. And everything we do is very visual—from the food to the cart to the trucks and the brick-and-mortar, and this book.

Eventually, themes started to emerge in the food. With all the great produce around, I started being drawn to vegetables that you wouldn't usually see in a taco—sweet potato, cauliflower, eggplant, Zuckerman farms asparagus, celery root, sunchokes, beets. Which places make tacos like that? And I made them with some flavor. I made them hefty. The challenge for a chef trying to do this type of taco is not to just dress veggies with sour cream because they're light. I had to find ways to highlight and complement those vegetables with other ingredients.

If you're using a light vegetable, cook with a lot of rich butter. Nuts in salsas can add heft. Dry fruits complement nuts well. Dry herbs pair well with complementary cheeses, which add a component of fat. We aren't trying to be vegetarian or vegan.

But I don't want to be bored cooking the same proteins over and again just because I'm doing tacos. Vegetables are cheaper and better for the environment, and you can get some of the best vegetables in the world here in Los Angeles, year-round.

Another theme that emerged was local seafood. At first I'd try to get more obscure and pricy things just to be cool and chef-y. But then I eventually moved over to focusing on what's best that's here. Santa Barbara sea urchin—it's the best in the world you can get, and it's from just a few miles away. We offer it at a more affordable price than anywhere else it's available on the planet, and it's almost always on the menu. Now I don't look for anything pricy. I just get what's best that's local and serve it all the time.

Experimenting with chiles and different salsa making was fun for me and I developed a similar philosophy of using what's here. Switching out sesames for cashews, pine nuts for almonds, raisins for dates. Why shy away from products that we have in plenty? Eventually we came up with a local style. Some have called it "Alta California." It's very much tied to Los Angeles traditions, the diversity of the people who live here, and the amazing selection of our farmers' markets. Like when we went to Mexico as a pop-up, our food totally changed; they didn't have sweet potatoes, so I used pumpkin and created a new taco we love serving. And the market I went to also didn't have wild baby arugula, but they had this other spicy bitter herb, so that came into the food.

The unfortunate thing is that in some places you won't find everything we have here in L.A., but that's what's made our food what it is. You don't have to scour the city to find an obscure ingredient from Oaxaca, just use what you have that's equal to it in the same way. Keep the basic tenets: spicy should stay spicy, sweet should stay sweet, and so on. Cape gooseberries are in the same family as tomatillos, so why not make a gooseberry salsa? Or, try making a cooked salsa with all raw ingredients, and vice versa. Experiment. Not everything will work but tomorrow you can try something new. That's the great freedom of our food that we've kept from the cart to the truck.

The only two consistent items on the menu on the truck are always a sweet potato taco and always some kind of tostada. At the future brick-and-mortar restaurant, we just want to upgrade. We'll have six or seven consistent items—sweet potato, oxtail, cauliflower, pocho, and fried potato tacos; ahi poke tostada; and a breakfast burrito—and two or three specials. Something seasonal or something rare. We are going to have to make a lot of mistakes. We're going to have a rotisserie spit so we can experiment. Cooking vegetables and different proteins on a spit is one idea we're tossing around that would be something totally different.

We're going to have a full liquor license at the brick-and-mortar, so we want to do cocktails. We're not going to do small share plates or tapas. We're going to do big plates if we're suggesting sharing. I'd like to do some stuff where you sit with your friends and there's a big pan of octopus cooked with chorizo and some tortillas on the side. It'll give us a chance to serve a family-style thing. That will be new for us, because at this point all the tacos, including salsas and garnishes, have always been made to order.

It's going to evolve a little bit from where we are on the truck. We're different now than we were a year ago, and two years ago, and we're going to be so different a year from now. There isn't really a business plan we can write for this. It's just about evolving.

Why not do everything imaginable?

FRIENDS OF GUERRILLA TACOS

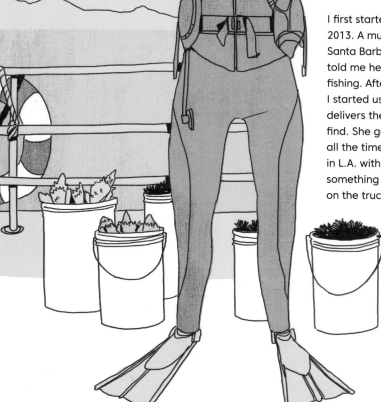

These are some of the most passionate shepherds of their respective crafts that I've come across. Each one shares a drive to provide the best possible product to their clients. Actually, I wouldn't just consider them vendors, I'd say they're friends and partners. All of these people are at the top of their game and we couldn't do what we do without them.

STEPHANIE MUTZ
OF SEA STEPHANIE FISH

I first started working with Stephanie Mutz in 2013. A mutual friend, Drake Whitcraft out of Santa Barbara (shout out, Whitcraft Winery!), told me he knew someone who did local fishing. After I tasted what Stephanie caught, I started using her product. Every week, she delivers the freshest local seafood you can find. She gets me the best uni, and I use it all the time. She supplies tons of restaurants in L.A. with fantastic uni, and it's definitely something we almost always have available on the truck. Shout out to Stephanie!

TOSHIHIDE KAWAI OF LUXE SEAFOOD

Kawai was one of the first vendors to sell to me. Being as small as I was, whatever I needed, Luxe was always there to help me source the best seafood. Whenever they get something special, I'll get a text at 5:30 a.m. telling me what's coming in. I've always appreciated their commitment to providing the best product from around the world. I'll get blood clams and chocolate clams, yellowfin tuna, spiny lobsters, abalone—all great quality. Thank you, Kawai!

KRYS COOK OF COOK PIGS RANCH

While stalking heritage pork on Instagram, I came across Cook Pigs Ranch's page. When I clicked to go to their website, I discovered they were pasture-raising pigs in a very humane manner that's very similar to the way the Spanish raise the black pigs in Andalusia. So after cold-calling Krys, she invited me to come up to her ranch to see what she does. I came back from the ranch with the best pork chop I'd ever had. I was sold.

ROASTED PUMPKIN TACO

Recently while doing Guerrilla Tacos pop-ups in Mexico City, we were challenged to use only ingredients that were available seasonally at the market. I saw a pumpkin and immediately remembered seeing a whole pumpkin charred in a wood-fired oven at Pazar in Australia. And so this taco was invented on the spot.

This also includes a very spicy salsa. The reason we use such a spicy salsa with this dish is because there are a lot of sweet components, and we need to cut the sweetness with some spice. If you don't have a mortar and pestle, a food processor will work fine.

Bird's Beak Salsa

1 cup Thai or bird's beak chiles, or about 15 small colorful chiles

2 garlic cloves, peeled and thinly sliced

¼ cup white vinegar

Kosher salt

Pear Vinaigrette

1 tablespoon unsalted butter

1 pear, cored and cut into thin slices

1 tablespoon honey

1 tablespoon Dijon mustard

½ cup champagne vinegar

1 cup grapeseed oil

Kosher salt

2 cups crushed pecans

¼ cup light corn syrup

¼ cup granulated sugar

2 tablespoons whole cumin seeds

2½ tablespoons kosher salt

1 cup golden raisins or dried figs

2½ cups fresh orange juice

¼ cup mezcal

To make the bird's beak salsa: In a mortar and pestle, pound together the chiles and garlic. Really pound it! You should see a paste forming. Keep going. You want it fully pulverized, but you're doing it by hand. After you're getting close, slowly incorporate the white vinegar. Season with salt and set aside.

To make the pear vinaigrette: In a 12-inch cast-iron skillet over medium-high heat, melt the butter until it's nicely browned, not black. Add the pear and caramelize thoroughly, about 6 minutes. Then add the honey and, using a heatproof spatula, scrape up the browned bits from the bottom of the pan. Cook for 2 to 3 minutes, just to warm through, and then set aside to cool. In a blender, combine the pear, mustard, champagne vinegar, and grapeseed oil; puree thoroughly; and season with salt. Set aside.

Preheat the oven to 325°F. Line a baking sheet with a silicone mat.

In a medium mixing bowl, toss together the pecans, corn syrup, granulated sugar, cumin seeds, and ½ tablespoon of the salt. Transfer to the prepared baking sheet and roast for about 8 minutes, or until golden brown. Remove from the oven and set aside to cool. Once thoroughly cooled, break up the pecans with your hands and set aside.

In a saucepan over high heat, combine the raisins, orange juice, and mezcal. Let the mixture reduce until the raisins soak up 90 percent of the juice. They should be plump. Set aside.

continued

Turn a gas grill to 500°F or use a charcoal grill and light as many coals as it takes to make a pile several inches wider in diameter than your pumpkin and that reaches within an inch or two of the grate.

Place the whole pumpkin as close to the fire (or hot coals) as you can. Blacken thoroughly, flipping to get it blackened evenly all around, about 25 minutes. Then, use a thin knife to pierce the pumpkin to make sure it's cooked through. You should get some resistance from the skin, but the knife should slide into the flesh smoothly after that. You should be able to put the knife in and pull it out without too much effort. Remove the pumpkin from the fire and let rest for about 5 minutes.

Preheat the oven to 425°F.

Begin peeling all the black parts off the pumpkin. Cut the pumpkin in half vertically, and remove and discard the seeds and fibers. Cut the pumpkin into wedges and portion into 3-by-2-inch pieces about ¾ inch thick. (These don't have to be uniform; you just want them to be able to fit in the tortillas.) Place the cut pieces into a 12-by-24-inch roasting pan and brush melted butter liberally over each. Sprinkle with the remaining 2 tablespoons salt, the pepper, thyme, and brown sugar. Roast for 15 to 20 minutes, or until golden brown. Set aside.

In a mixing bowl, combine the arugula, raisins, pecans, goat cheese, and pear vinaigrette so it's almost like a salad.

Top the tortillas with a layer of the roasted pumpkin, then the arugula mixture, and finally the salsa. Serve immediately.

One 3- to 4-pound pumpkin, blue hubbard, winter squash, or butternut squash

1 cup unsalted butter, melted

1 tablespoon freshly ground black pepper

10 thyme sprigs

1 cup brown sugar

6 cups baby or wild arugula

1 cup goat cheese, crumbled

12 corn tortillas, warmed (see page 29)

CELERY ROOT TACO

This is a good winter taco. I enjoy the flavor of celery, especially in this form, because a celery root is milder than a celery stalk. The mixture of the greens with the apple and pistachio is a great way to round out one of the heartier vegetable tacos I make.

2 celery roots, peeled and cut into 1-inch cubes

Kosher salt

3 tablespoons unsalted butter

1 Fuji or other tart firm apple, cored and cut into eighths

4 stalks Swiss chard, ribs removed, greens torn into 2-by-2-inch pieces

2 tablespoons dried cranberries

2 tablespoons raw, unsalted, shelled pistachios

Freshly ground black pepper

1 lemon, halved

1 garlic clove, smashed under the side of a knife

8 corn tortillas, warmed (see page 29)

Burnt Tomato Salsa (page 38) for topping

¼ cup torn celery leaves, yellow part only

Fill a 4-quart stockpot with cold water, add the celery roots, and place over high heat until the water boils. Season with 1 tablespoon salt and lower the temperature to a medium simmer. Cook for 8 minutes. Pierce a piece of celery root with a knife—it should have the texture of a cooked potato. Once it's fully cooked, drain and discard the water. Set aside.

In a 10-inch cast-iron skillet over medium-high heat, melt 2 tablespoons of the butter. Once the butter is bubbling, add the apple, placing the slices on their sides, and season with a pinch of salt. Cook, moving the slices occasionally to make sure they don't burn, for 4 minutes, or until they are mostly cooked and getting golden brown. Turn the apples to cook the other side for about 2 minutes. Add all the Swiss chard and stir. Cook for 3 minutes, then add the cranberries. Cook for another 1 minute. Add the pistachios and cook for 2 minutes more. Season with salt and pepper and remove from the heat. Squeeze the lemon over the top and set aside.

In an 8-inch cast-iron skillet over medium-high heat, melt the remaining 1 tablespoon butter. When it's bubbling, add the celery root and cook for about 3 minutes, until it's golden brown. Add the garlic and continue cooking for another 2 minutes.

Divide the browned celery root among the tortillas. Top with the apple–Swiss chard mixture and salsa and garnish with the celery leaves. Serve immediately.

CORN TACO

When lobster mushrooms and corn are available at the same time, I like to pair them because the sweetness of the corn plays well off the earthiness of the mushrooms. We do these on the grill. We're just looking for a little bit of that grill flavor, so we're not going straight onto the coals. You're going to need 15 wooden clothespins soaked in water for about 45 minutes to hold the tacos closed while grilling.

Chile Morita Salsa

1 tablespoon vegetable oil

3 dried chiles morita, stemmed and seeded

2 dried chiles cascabels, stemmed and seeded

1 pound tomatillos, preferably milperos, husked and rinsed

2 garlic cloves, peeled

2 tablespoons pepitas (pumpkin seeds)

1 teaspoon cumin seeds

¼ cup white vinegar

Kosher salt

Kosher salt

1 pinch of sugar

Kernels from 4 ears Brentwood corn (sweet yellow corn)

2 pounds peewee or fingerling potatoes

¼ cup unsalted butter, plus 1 cup at room temperature

3 garlic cloves, peeled and sliced

To make the chile morita salsa: In a 10-inch cast-iron skillet over medium heat, warm the vegetable oil. Add all the chiles and toast until aromatic, about 45 seconds. Then add the tomatillos, garlic, pepitas, and cumin seeds and cook until the tomatillos are soft and break apart easily with the back of a spoon. Slide the contents of the skillet into a blender, add the vinegar, and blend well. Taste and season with salt. Set aside.

In a 4-quart saucepan over high heat, bring 2 quarts water to a boil. Add salt until it's as salty as the sea. Then, add the sugar and corn kernels and cook for 5 minutes. Drain the water and set the corn aside.

In the same saucepan over high heat, bring another 2 quarts water to a boil. Add salt until it's as salty as the sea. Add the potatoes and cook until a knife can slide through one with no resistance, about 8 minutes.

In a 12-inch cast-iron skillet over medium-high heat, melt the ¼ cup butter. Add the garlic and sauté until aromatic, about 2 minutes. Then add the mushrooms and thyme and cook for about 7 minutes, until the mushrooms cook down and turn slightly golden brown in places. Turn off the heat and season well with salt. Remove the thyme.

Mix the corn, potatoes, and mushrooms with the remaining 1 cup butter.

Stuff each tortilla with about 3 tablespoons of the corn-potato-mushroom mixture. Fold the tortillas together at the top and pinch them closed with soaked clothespins. The tortillas should absorb a lot of the butter, which will help them toast and roast over the fire.

Prepare a medium fire in a charcoal grill, heat a gas grill to medium, or set a cast-iron grill over medium-high heat.

Lay the tacos flat on their sides and face them all in the same direction. They should get a little blackened and very toasted. Turn them over after 3 minutes. The second side won't need as long, maybe 1½ minutes. They should get a little crispy and slightly burnt.

Place the tacos on a big platter and douse well all over with the salsa. Serve immediately.

1 pound lobster mushrooms, cleaned thoroughly and sliced into ½-inch-thick pieces (uneven pieces are okay and even encouraged)

1 bunch of thyme

15 corn tortillas, warmed (see page 29)

WILD BOAR TACO

Wild boar is a little sweeter and a little gamier than ground beef, and a little leaner than ground pork. It's fun to work with and is just a little bit of a variation on what you'd normally get out of your everyday proteins. This taco is pretty similar to our Pocho Taco (page 38), but it's not fried and we add the *rajas* (chiles). I love coastal cheddar with this, it's super-sharp and rich and nutty.

8 Anaheim chiles

½ tablespoon vegetable oil

2 pounds ground boar meat or ground lamb, beef, or chicken

Kosher salt

¼ cup minced shallots

½ cup finely diced yellow onion

1 serrano chile, with seeds, stemmed and chopped

¾ teaspoon ground cumin

½ tablespoon garlic powder

½ tablespoon onion powder

¼ cup pine nuts

15 corn tortillas, warmed (see page 29)

½ recipe Lemon Crema (page 38)

10 ounces aged cheddar, preferably an English coastal cheddar, roughly broken into 2-inch pieces

1 cup cherry tomatoes, washed and halved

¼ cup torn micro cilantro leaves

On the stove top, roast the Anaheims until blackened but not ash-gray, about 4 minutes. Remove from the heat, place in a food-safe ziplock bag, and let steam for 5 minutes. Then, remove from the bag and, with a kitchen napkin, slide off the blackened skins. Slice the chiles in half vertically, discard the cores and seeds, and cut lengthwise into fajita-size slices, about 1 by 4 inches. Set aside.

In a 12-inch cast-iron skillet over medium heat, warm the vegetable oil. Add the meat and let brown, breaking it up with a wooden spoon as you go. Season with salt. Using a slotted spoon, transfer the meat to a plate but leave the fat in the pan.

Add the shallots, onion, and serrano to the rendered fat and sauté over medium heat until the onion is translucent, about 3 minutes. Add the cumin, garlic powder, onion powder, and pine nuts; stir; and cook for another 3 to 5 minutes, until crispy but not burnt. Add the meat and roasted Anaheims and stir until fully mixed and heated through.

Add a scoop of the meat mixture to each tortilla; top with 1 tablespoon crema, a few pieces of cheese, and a scattering of cherry tomatoes; and then garnish with the cilantro. Serve immediately.

chard   8:12:39

October 27

1 × **Wild Boar**
----
1 × -------------------------

1 × **Wild Boar**
        No spice   wesley's iPad

        Receipt FXPu

OXTAIL TACO

One of the most memorable oxtails I've ever had was in Madrid. After the bullfights, Tanya and I walked up the avenue to find one of the restaurants that served *rabo del torro* (oxtails), and after tasting it, it became one of my favorite cuts of beef, period. I sometimes take it over the top with a slice of seared foie gras. It's a delicious luxury.

1 whole oxtail, or about 5 pounds cut oxtail, fatty white parts trimmed off (see Note, opposite)

Kosher salt

Freshly ground black pepper

½ cup vegetable oil

1 cup diced yellow onion

½ cup peeled and diced carrot

½ cup diced celery

4 thyme sprigs

2 bay leaves

2 tablespoons balsamic vinegar

2½ cups tawny port

One 750-ml bottle hearty red wine

4 flat-leaf parsley sprigs

4 cups beef stock

Raw Avocado-Tomatillo Salsa

1 pound tomatillos (preferably tomatillos milperos, the small purple ones about the size of a quarter), husked and rinsed

2 avocados, pitted, peeled, and chopped

2 serrano chiles,

6 garlic cloves, peeled

1 bunch of cilantro, with 2 inches of stem ends removed

Kosher salt

4 to 6 limes

Remove the oxtail from the refrigerator an hour before cooking and allow to come to room temperature. Season generously with salt and pepper on all sides.

Preheat the oven to 275°F.

Put a Dutch oven over high heat for 3 minutes. Add the vegetable oil and wait a minute or two, until the pan is very hot, almost smoking, then add the oxtail (in batches if necessary) and sear until nicely browned on all three meaty sides. Do not crowd the meat or get lazy or rushed at this step; it will take about 15 minutes. Remove the oxtail from the pan and set aside on a large platter or in a bowl until ready to continue cooking.

Turn the heat to medium and add the onion, carrot, celery, thyme, and bay leaves. Stir with a wooden spoon, scraping up all the crusty bits in the pan. Cook for 6 to 8 minutes, or until the vegetables just begin to caramelize. Add the balsamic vinegar, port, red wine, and parsley. Turn the heat to high and reduce the liquid by half. Add the beef stock and bring to a boil.

Place the oxtails in the stock mixture. Cover with a lid and cook in the oven for 8 hours.

To make the avocado-tomatillo salsa: In a food processor, combine the tomatillos, avocados, serranos, garlic, cilantro, and 1 tablespoon salt. Juice the limes on top. Cover and hit it three or four times—pop, pop, pop—then let it blend a while. You'll start to see the seeds. Keep it chunky though. Taste it and season with more salt. Set aside.

To make the pickled onions: In a stockpot over medium heat, combine the red wine vinegar and water. Add the sugar and salt, then add the mustard seeds, coriander seeds, chile, cinnamon stick, peppercorns, and star anise. Cook for about 10 minutes, then remove from the heat and add the onion. Let sit for about 1 hour. (Store in an airtight container in the refrigerator for up to 1 week.)

When the oxtails are done, strain the liquid into a saucepan and reduce over medium-high heat until the sauce thickens enough to coat the back of the spoon. Put the spoon in the liquid and wipe a finger across it—a line should appear with the sauce gently spreading. If the sauce doesn't move or is too sticky, you've gone too far. If that happens, add a bit of broth to thin it out.

Try to gently split the meat from the oxtail bones, it will be easier to gently remove the tail if it's whole. Don't shred the meat—cut it into little pieces. We aren't making machaca; we don't want it stringy. (We save the bones for our dog, Pono, or you can throw them out.)

Put the meat back into the saucepan with the sauce and heat until it's hot. Taste it and add salt if needed. You're just mixing it together and reheating it a bit. There should be just enough sauce to more than coat the meat.

Layer some oxtail, some pickled onions, and then some salsa in each tortilla and sprinkle some chives on top. Serve immediately.

NOTE If you have a whole oxtail, try to cook it whole. If it's too big to fit in your pan, you'll need to cut it down. After you trim off the fat, cut into one of the joints with your knife. Choose the position of the joint so that you're ending up with pieces that will fit into your pan. You should feel a lock into the joint. If you feel bone, wedge the knife back and forth until it gives—that's the cartilage and that's where you cut through.

Pickled Onions

½ cup red wine vinegar

1 cup water

¼ cup sugar

1 tablespoon kosher salt

2 tablespoons mustard seeds

1 tablespoon coriander seeds

1 dried chile de árbol, stemmed

½ cinnamon stick

8 black peppercorns

1 star anise

2 cups very thinly sliced red onion

12 corn tortillas, warmed (see page 29)

1 bunch of chives, minced

DUCK HEART TACO

Where are you going to get duck hearts? I don't know. Use the Internet! I get mine at Gourmet Imports in Los Angeles. I buy them by the 5-pound bag. My minimum order is 80 pounds. It almost tastes like soujouk, the Armenian sausage. This is the same way I prepare turkey neck, and similar to how I do carnitas. It all comes from Thomas Keller's duck confit. You use a lot of herbs with salt and then you remove all the excess liquid. The hearts don't absorb the fat so easily but if you salt them up, the texture works much better and the process removes a lot of the liquid, that is, the blood, and therefore, the blood flavor. If you don't salt them up, then you'll get a little coagulated blood on your tacos. I'm not too down for that.

The difference between this recipe and my carnitas is with this one you're adding fat.

Carrot-Gooseberry Salsa

1 cup peeled and diagonally sliced carrots

4 habanero chiles

2 garlic cloves

1 cup gooseberries

¼ cup white vinegar

Kosher salt

Green Salt (page 79)

32 duck hearts

Pickled Persimmons

6 fuyu persimmons (choose very firm fruit; if it's too ripe the fruit will turn to jam when you add the pickling liquid)

1½ cups water

1 cup apple cider vinegar

½ cup sugar

1 teaspoon coriander seeds

1 teaspoon mustard seeds

1 teaspoon black peppercorns

3 allspice berries

To make the carrot-gooseberry salsa: In a blender, combine the carrots, habaneros, garlic, gooseberries, and white vinegar and blend until totally smooth. Season with salt. It should be very spicy. Set aside.

Use your hands to rub the green salt all over the duck hearts and place the hearts on a wire rack set on a plate. Place in the fridge, uncovered, for at least 4 hours or up to overnight. You should see some red liquid coming off of the hearts, not much, but some.

To make the pickled persimmons: While the hearts are in the fridge, remove the green stems from the persimmons and halve the fruit lengthwise. Cut each half into wedges.

In a saucepan over high heat, combine the water and cider vinegar and bring to a boil. Add the sugar, coriander seeds, mustard seeds, peppercorns, allspice, clove, star anise, chile de árbol, bay leaf, and cinnamon and boil for 5 minutes. Turn off the heat, add the persimmons, and let sit for about 1 hour. Store in an airtight container in the fridge for up to 2 months.

Preheat the oven to 225°F.

In a small pot over medium heat, warm the duck fat until it's liquid. You don't want it too hot; just liquid enough so that you can pour it.

Remove the hearts from the fridge, rinse thoroughly, and pat dry with paper towels. Place the hearts in a small roasting pan. Try to get them in a single layer, but it's okay if you can't. Pour the duck fat over the duck hearts; they should be covered entirely. Now, add the garlic and 6 thyme sprigs and roast for 5 hours.

Using a slotted spoon, remove the hearts from the roasting pan and place on a pan or plate to drain. Eat one—the texture should have a little bit of a bite to it. Almost like a chicken oyster. It should be pretty well seasoned. Cut them in half lengthwise.

In a 12-inch cast-iron skillet over medium-high heat, sear the duck hearts with the remaining 2 thyme sprigs until the hearts are very aromatic and slightly browned. Add the pistachios; the residual fat of the hearts should be enough to sauté them. When they get a little crispy and golden brown, and are a little toasted, you're done. Keep warm. Discard the thyme.

Put about eight pieces of duck heart on each tortilla. Add one or two slices of pickled persimmon, the salsa (as much as you want, but it's very spicy), and garnish with the parsley and fresh dill. Serve immediately.

1 whole clove

1 star anise

1 dried chile de árbol

1 bay leaf

½ cinnamon stick

3 cups duck fat

6 garlic cloves, smashed with the side of a knife,

8 thyme sprigs

2 tablespoons crushed raw, unsalted, shelled pistachios

8 corn tortillas, warmed (see page 29)

2 tablespoons fresh flat-leaf parsley leaves torn from stems

2 tablespoons fresh dill leaves, torn from stems

PORK BELLY AND CAVIAR TACO

Pork belly is one of my favorite things, especially when it comes from Cook Pigs Ranch in Julian, California. And all caviar is good. So I wanted to have some fun and do a surf-and-turf taco. This is one of my favorite surfs with one of my favorite turfs.

2 pounds pork belly, skin-on, single piece, scored with 1-by-1-inch crosshatches about ½ inch apart on the skin side

2 carrots, peeled and diced into large pieces

1 yellow onion, diced into large pieces

3 stalks celery, ends removed, diced into large pieces

2 bay leaves

8 black peppercorns

1 bunch of flat-leaf parsley

3 thyme sprigs

1 star anise

2 garlic cloves

One 750-ml bottle dry white wine

Kosher salt

Freshly ground black pepper

9 corn tortillas, warmed (see page 29)

Roasted Habanero-Serrano Salsa (page 47) for topping

2 ounces caviar, any kind

¼ cup minced fresh chives

Grated zest of 1 Meyer lemon

Preheat the oven to 325°F.

In a large roasting pan, combine the pork (skin-side up), carrots, onion, celery, bay leaves, peppercorns, parsley, thyme, star anise, garlic, and wine. Season with salt and cover with oven-safe plastic wrap and aluminum foil. Roast for 8 hours.

Line a baking sheet with parchment paper or plastic wrap and sprinkle with salt and pepper. Place the cooked belly on it (discard the liquid and spices). Season the top with salt and pepper and wrap directly with plastic wrap. Place a second baking sheet on top and stack with weights and put in the fridge. Leave it like this for at least 4 hours or up to overnight. This will compress the pork belly and make it much easier to cook evenly. When you're ready to eat, cut the meat into 3-by-½-inch slices.

Set a 12-inch cast-iron skillet over medium-high heat. Add the pork belly and cook until golden brown, then season with salt.

Layer the pork belly on the tortillas. Top with salsa, a small dollop of caviar, minced chives, and lemon zest. Serve immediately.

OCTOPUS AND CHORIZO TACO

This is another really good example of surf and turf done well. I think the meatiness of the octopus lends itself well to absorbing the chorizo when you cook them together. It reminds me a little of the Spanish dish calamari with chorizo, from the first restaurant I ever worked at.

Fill a 6-quart pot with 3 quarts water and add the onion, celery, coriander seeds, 1 tablespoon salt, and octopi. Bring to a boil and then lower the heat to a simmer. Cook for 5 hours, then remove the octopi and discard the cooking liquid and vegetables. Cut the octopi in half, lengthwise.

In a 10-inch cast-iron skillet over medium-high heat, render the chorizo for 3 to 4 minutes, breaking it up with a wooden spoon as you go. Add the octopi and let brown, about 2 minutes. Add the tomatoes and let blister, about 2 minutes. Season with salt and pepper. Add the pistachios and toss a few times to evenly distribute.

Divide the octopi among the tortillas, squeeze some lemon juice on top, top with salsa, and sprinkle on some chives. Serve immediately.

½ red onion, diced

½ cup diced celery

1 tablespoon coriander seeds

Kosher salt

2 pounds whole baby octopi, cleaned

4 ounces chorizo (see page 54)

½ cup cherry tomatoes

Freshly ground black pepper

4 cups whole raw, unsalted, shelled pistachios

4 corn tortillas, warmed (see page 29)

2 lemons, halved

Raw Tomatillo Salsa (page 160) for topping

Minced chives for sprinkling

Thyme sprigs for garnishing

FRIED CLAM TACO

When I first visited the city of Marbella in Spain, there were many fry stands that served fried fish, fried shrimp, all kinds of fried seafood. This became my favorite casual way to eat seafood, with a squeeze of lemon. I love showcasing the flavor of the clam in this taco with a super-spicy salsa. Please make sure to order shucked Ipswich clams with bellies.

Shiso Aïoli

1 egg yolk

2 white anchovies

3 garlic cloves, peeled

Juice of 1 lemon, or as needed

9 dashes Tabasco sauce

4 dashes Worchestershire sauce

8 shiso leaves

1 cup vegetable oil

Kosher salt

4 cups vegetable oil

1 cup all-purpose flour

1 tablespoon Old Bay Seasoning

Kosher salt

8 cups buttermilk

1 cup almond flour

2 pounds shucked Ipswich clams

12 corn tortillas, warmed
(see page 29)

Salsa del Valle (page 133)
for topping

¼ cup torn micro parsley leaves

½ cup crushed Marcona almonds

2 lemons, cut into wedges

To make the shiso aïoli: In a blender, combine the egg yolk, anchovies, garlic, lemon juice, Tabasco, Worcestershire, and shiso leaves and blend on low-medium speed. Begin adding the vegetable oil slowly and keep adding until you have a consistency a bit thinner than mayo. Adjust the seasoning with salt and lemon juice. Store in an airtight container in the fridge for up to 1 week.

In a 12-inch cast-iron skillet with high sides, heat the 4 cups vegetable oil to 360°F.

In a baking dish, mix together the all-purpose flour, Old Bay, and 2 tablespoons salt. In a separate dish, pour in the buttermilk. In a third dish, pour in the almond flour. Set them next to the stove.

First, dip the clams in the all-purpose flour mixture, then in the buttermilk, then in the almond flour, and drop them into the hot oil, being careful not to crowd the pan. Fry the clams until they are golden brown, 3 to 5 minutes. Remove them with a slotted spoon and place on a wire rack. Season with salt immediately.

Spread 1 tablespoon aïoli on each tortilla and top each with 3 or 4 clams and some salsa. Garnish with the parsley and almonds and squeeze lemon juice over the tops. Serve immediately.

SERVES 4 (3 TAQUITOS EACH)

PUERTO VALLARTA–STYLE CRAB TAQUITO

This taquito was inspired by a trip to Puerto Vallarta. Most seafood restaurants there have a *taco de jaiba* (crab taco) on their menus, and this is just my version of that delicious dish. It's almost more of an enchilada than a taco. They call it a taco, but I'm going to call it a taquito. Of course, they don't use Old Bay, either.

1 tablespoon lard, or as needed

7 guajillo chiles, stemmed

2 dried California chiles, stemmed

1 cup diced yellow onion

9 Roma tomatoes, cored and halved lengthwise

1 teaspoon ground cumin

2 allspice berries

1 whole clove

1 tablespoon pepitas (pumpkin seeds)

1 cup apple cider vinegar

½ cup water

Kosher salt

1 pound cooked crabmeat

2 shallots, minced

3 garlic cloves, peeled and minced

1 tablespoon Old Bay seasoning

1 tablespoon dried parsley

¼ cup extra-virgin olive oil

12 corn tortillas, warmed (see page 29)

½ cup unsalted butter

In a cast-iron skillet over high heat, melt the lard. Add all the chiles and toast until aromatic, about 1 minute. Remove the chiles from the pan, lower the heat to medium, and add the onion. Cook until the onion is translucent, about 3 minutes. Add the tomatoes and cook until soft, about 8 minutes. Then, return the chiles to the skillet along with the cumin, allspice, clove, and pepitas. If you feel it needs more lard at any point because it's drying out or burning, add some. Cook for 10 minutes and then remove from the heat. Transfer the contents of the skillet to a blender, add the vinegar and water, and puree until totally smooth. Season with salt and set aside.

In a large mixing bowl, combine one-fourth of the chile-tomato mixture, the crabmeat, shallots, garlic, Old Bay, parsley, and olive oil and stir to mix thoroughly. Season with salt.

Roll 2 or 3 tablespoons of crab filling into each tortilla. This should make about 12 taquitos.

In a 12-inch cast-iron skillet over medium to medium-high heat, melt 2 tablespoons of the butter until it coats the pan. Place three taquitos in the skillet, snug up next to each other, folded-side down, and sear. You want them more than golden brown. The sides of the tortillas should almost stick together. Once they're nicely browned, use the largest spatula you have to gently flip them over, all three at once. They should be sticking together, if not, no worries, you can flip them one at a time. Once you flip them,

continued

pour half of the chile-tomato mixture on top of the taquitos. The oil and the liquid of the tomatoes will react like when you throw water into a hot pan. Cook these down for another 3 to 4 minutes with the sauce, until the sauce is incorporated. Transfer the taquitos to a serving plate. Repeat with the remaining butter, taquitos, and chile-tomato mixture, working as fast as you can.

Top the taquitos with a dollop of crema, cover liberally with salsa, and garnish with torn cilantro. Serve immediately.

Dijon Crema (page 44) for topping

Avocado-Tomatillo Salsa (page 76) for covering

1 cup cilantro leaves, torn from stems

TURKEY NECK CONFIT BURRITO

A turkey neck doesn't yield much meat so you'll need four turkey necks, which you can find in L.A. at Super King. Of course, around Thanksgiving, you can also get the turkey necks from your friends—because everybody's about to cook a turkey, but they ain't gonna do nothing with those necks. At least, I doubt they'll be doing turkey neck confit, and turkey neck confit is super-delicious in this burrito.

Usually with Guerrilla Tacos' confits, we use a green salt of fresh bay, parsley, and thyme, à la Thomas Keller, and let the moisture drain off the meat overnight, but we're not gonna use the green salt for this because it isn't necessary with a turkey neck. The difference between a turkey neck and a duck heart or even a piece of pork shoulder is, for whatever reason, you don't need to remove any extra moisture.

Plus, we're basically making a machaca out of the necks. We only confit the necks to get the meat, which then is shredded and sautéed, off of the bone. You can use this for a burrito or taco but it's super-good in this very simple burrito. This is just meat, salsa, and a little cilantro. Use the best large flour tortillas you can find. It's simple, and it's the fucking bomb.

Roasted Tomatillo Salsa

1 pound tomatillos, husked, rinsed, and halved if larger than a silver dollar

½ cup sliced yellow or white onion

2 garlic cloves, peeled

1 serrano chile, stemmed

1 poblano chile, stemmed, seeded, and sliced

Vegetable oil for drizzling

Kosher salt

Juice from 2 limes

To make the roasted tomatillo salsa: Place a rack at the highest possible position in your oven and preheat the broiler.

Put the tomatillos, onion, garlic, and both chiles on a large baking sheet. Drizzle lightly with vegetable oil, season with salt, and gently toss with your hands to lightly coat the vegetables. Broil for 10 minutes, remove from the oven and toss the vegetables once with a spatula, then broil for another 5 minutes. You're looking for the vegetables to be nicely roasted and slightly blackened in spots.

Slide the contents of the baking sheet into a food processor and pulse until chunky but not liquified or fully blended. There should be chunks of the chiles and flecks of roasted skin. Add the lime juice and pulse once more to incorporate. Season with salt. Set aside.

Preheat the oven to 225°F.

In a small pot over medium heat, warm the duck fat until it's liquid. You don't want it too hot; just liquid enough so that you can pour it.

Rinse the turkey necks under cold running water. Pat them dry with paper towels and season liberally with salt and pepper.

In a 12-inch cast-iron skillet, lay the necks flat along with the whole garlic cloves, thyme, and peppercorns. Cover with the duck fat, transfer to the oven, and roast for at least 8 hours or up to overnight.

Remove the skillet from the oven. Using a slotted spoon, remove the necks from the fat and allow them to drain on a grate. Once they're cool enough to handle, using your hands, remove all the meat from the necks. The meat should slide right off. Discard the bones along with the garlic, thyme, and peppercorns, and pour all but 2 tablespoons of the fat into a separate container (reserve for another use or discard).

Place the skillet over medium-high heat, add the vegetable oil and onion and sauté until translucent, about 3 minutes, then add the sliced garlic. When the garlic is just aromatic, about 1 minute, add the jalapeño, tomatoes, bay leaves, chopped cilantro leaves, and cumin; season with salt and pepper; and cook for several minutes. When the tomatoes are very soft, add the turkey meat and stir with a spoon. Sauté until it's fully mixed and heated through and the flavors have had a chance to incorporate, about 5 minutes. Let it sit over the heat, without stirring, until there is a slight crispness to the turkey—maybe 2 to 3 minutes. Taste and season with salt and pepper, if desired, and then remove the pan from the heat.

Spoon some of the turkey mix into each tortilla, add as much salsa as you want, and garnish with the rough-chopped cilantro and stems. Roll up your burritos and enjoy.

3 cups duck fat, or enough to cover the necks (use lard if you can't find duck fat)

4 turkey necks

Kosher salt

Freshly ground black pepper

5 garlic cloves; 3 thinly sliced

4 thyme sprigs

8 peppercorns

1 tablespoon vegetable oil

1 white onion, julienned

1 jalapeño chile, thinly sliced into coins

4 Roma tomatoes, quartered

2 bay leaves

1 cup chopped fresh cilantro leaves, plus 1 cup rough-chopped cilantro, stems included

1 teaspoon ground cumin

2 large flour tortillas, the best you can find, warmed (see page 29)

TOSTADAS: A GUIDE

The tostada is like the tortilla—it's just a vessel. Making a tostada is easy. You don't have to think too much. You just need the right ingredients in the right proportion.

Tostadas can have any topping, meat, or vegetable, but for me, a tostada starts with choosing what kind of fish to use. On the truck, some stuff is more stable so we end up using more of those types of fish. Always get the best possible quality and the freshest fish available. With fish, there's not much you can do to cheat it. That's the beautiful simplicity and key to any tostada. A tostada should be both light and filling. It's great to eat in the warmer months, which in Southern California is all the time. It's different than a lot of my food because, apart from the fried shell, there's very little, if any, fat. We might be using some finishing olive oil on it, but that's it.

FISH

You can use pretty much any fish preparation in a tostada—all sorts of tunas: ahi, big eye, albacore. Tuna is firm, not flaky, which makes it a good tostada ingredient. You can use other kinds of fish, too. You can use bass, you can use salmon. My favorite fish to eat raw is kampachi, otherwise known as almaco jack. It's fatty and the texture is better than albacore, which can be mealy. It just melts in your mouth. It's similar to yellowtail but it's better. The flesh of kampachi is almost white.

I tend to stay away from the hardcore oily fishier fish. But I like shellfish. Clams, certain raw shrimp, lobster—it's almost limitless. It's whatever you want to do. But personally, the one thing I wouldn't put on is an oyster. Something about the wetness of an oyster and the amount of oysters you'd need to put on a tostada seems gnarly to me. Plus the tostada shell would take on a lot of moisture and that would probably get unappetizing. For me, oysters are just meant to be raw, opened up, and eaten.

ACID

If you're eating your fish raw, you want some other ingredient that will add acidity. The acidity can come from either a salsa or fresh lime. We like to use Salsa Bruja (page 45) a lot. It is basically just enhanced lime juice. You're adding garlic and fish sauce and sugar, but the base is a lot of lime

juice. Then there's tons of umami you're adding to just kick it up but keeping it super-acidic.

FRUIT

Then, I think about fruit. Peaches, avocados, persimmons, raw apples—I've used kyoho grapes from the farmers' market. You want the fruit as firm as possible. White nectarines are great for this. Peaches—you want them just under-ripe. But nothing beats a white nectarine. Some argue watermelon is best and adds hydration, but watermelon is so hit and miss. Others say certain varieties of peak strawberries or perfectly ripe mulberries are best. But for me it's white nectarines. They're available July to September only, and that's the best time to be making tostadas.

SPICE

After fish and fruit, I think about adding some spiciness. I tend to use a lot of the raw tomatillo salsas because they have that acidity, with some added heat from fresh chiles. Usually there's nothing that's cooked in these salsas or in the tostada at all. I like the Salsa del Valle (page 133) we make because that uses a lot of oil. It coats nicely and also adds some fat when I'm working with a leaner fish. Sometimes you want a tostada totally coated in an oily salsa, but not always. Spice can also come from sliced chiles, which add some crunch.

TEXTURE

After fish, fruit, and spice, I think about texture. A tostada is brilliant because you have crunch from the shell. And I like using firmer fruits. But sometimes I'll add some extra crunch with pine nuts or sesame seeds or crushed almonds.

HERBS

You don't want to go too crazy with the herbs in tostadas. I lean heavily on chives and cilantro, but never dill. I like the brighter herbs. Shisho sometimes. Even cannabis leaves.

La Princesita
Tostada Norteña
USE BY
09 28 16
La Princesita
La Princesita

GOLDEN BEET POKE TOSTADA

I made this variation on a traditional poke for some vegan customers who always commented that the tuna poke looked really good. So this has the essence of the tuna poke but in a vegan version.

In a 4-quart saucepan over high heat, bring about 2 quarts water to a boil. Add salt until it's as salty as the sea. Drop in the beets and cook for about 40 minutes, or until soft enough to pierce with a knife with very little resistance. Remove the pan from the heat and, using a slotted spoon, remove the beets from the water. Using a paper towel, rub the skins off the beets, then use a paring knife to cut away any tough areas from the beets and cut the beets into 1-by-1-inch cubes. Refrigerate until cool, about 1 hour.

In a medium bowl, combine the miso, soy sauce, yuzu juice, sesame oil, and olive oil and stir until combined. Add the beets, toss with the soy mixture to coat well, and season with salt.

Using a slotted spoon, divide the beet mixture evenly among the tostada shells. Top with salsa del valle and raw tomatillo salsa. Shake the furikake over the top and garnish with the flowers, if desired. Serve immediately.

Kosher salt

6 beets, rinsed, tops and greens removed

2 tablespoons very good white miso (the most expensive kind is usually best)

¼ cup soy sauce

¼ cup yuzu juice

1 tablespoon sesame oil

1 tablespoon extra-virgin olive oil

8 tostada shells

Salsa del Valle (page 133) for topping

Raw Avocado-Tomatillo Salsa (page 214) for topping

3 tablespoons furikake

1 bunch of borage flowers or other small colorful edible flower, preferably purple or blue (optional)

RAZOR CLAM TOSTADA

I really love razor clams and enjoy them when they're simply steamed. But if you can get your hands on a fair amount of these, they make great tostadas. Since you don't get too much off of razor clams you need a good three clams for one tostada. But it's worth it.

Here in L.A., you can find razor clams at Luxe Seafood or Los Angeles Fish Company, when they're available. If you can't find razor clams in your area, consider ordering from a specialty fishmonger online.

1½ pounds razor clams (shells included)

3 tablespoons cornmeal

6 tablespoons extra-virgin olive oil

6 garlic cloves, smashed with the side of a knife

6 thyme sprigs

¼ cup Marcona almonds, crushed with the side of a knife

Juice of 1 lemon, plus 1 lemon, cut into wedges

Kosher salt

4 tostada shells

2 Pink Lady or other seasonal apples, halved and sliced very thinly, preferably with a mandoline

1 cup very thinly sliced (preferably with a mandoline) breakfast radishes

1 jalapeño chile, sliced very thinly, preferably with a mandoline

Avocado-Tomatillo Salsa (page 76) for drizzling

¼ cup chopped fresh cilantro

Place the razor clams in a pot standing with the shell openings up. (Razor clams are always slightly open.) Place the pot under the faucet and turn on the water to the lowest possible flow. Fill the pot with water and then keep the water running, overflowing into the sink. Sprinkle 1 tablespoon of the cornmeal into the pot about 1 minute later and keep the water running. The cornmeal helps the clams filter out the sand. After about 10 minutes, drain the water, rinse the pot, and repeat the process. Then repeat it again. You have to do it three times because razor clams are sandy. After three rinsings, the clams are ready to use.

Place a large (12-inch or greater) skillet over medium-high heat and coat with 2 tablespoons of the olive oil. Add as many clams as you can in a single layer; you want them flush with the pan. Depending on the size of your pan, you'll be working in batches; if you're using a 12-inch skillet, you'll be working in two batches. For the first batch, add half of the garlic and 3 thyme sprigs. Cover the pan and steam the clams for 4 minutes, or until they open wider. Remove the clams from the skillet and place on a baking sheet. Discard the garlic and thyme. Repeat with another 2 tablespoons olive oil and the remaining clams, garlic, and thyme.

Prepare an ice-water bath in the largest mixing bowl you have by stirring together water and a tray of ice.

continued

Remove the meat from the clam shells with your hands. Remove the belly (the meatiest part, about the size and shape of a finger) and discard the rest along with the shells. Rinse the clam bellies gently in the ice-water bath to make sure all the sand is gone—there could still be some sand, and you don't want a sandy tostada. Remove any entrails, dark bits, or anything but the white or cream-colored flesh of the clams. Slice the clams on the diagonal into pieces about ¾ inch in size.

In a mixing bowl, combine the clams, almonds, lemon juice, and remaining 2 tablespoons olive oil. Season with salt and gently mix.

Divide the clam mixture among the tostada shells, then add the apples, radishes, and jalapeño. You sort of decorate the clam mixture with the other ingredients, varying the ingredients and making it look natural. You're not doing like a layer of vegetables. Drizzle each with about 1½ tablespoons salsa and garnish with cilantro and a squeeze of lemon juice. Serve immediately.

SALMON TOSTADA

On one of my visits to Hawaii, I tasted a salmon dish called lomi-lomi. I really enjoyed it. It's very similar to poke, but with salmon. So I riffed on it and made my own version to serve on the truck.

2 tablespoons white miso

1 tablespoon white soy sauce

1 tablespoon yuzu juice

¼ cup extra-virgin olive oil

1 pound skinless salmon fillet, sliced into 1-inch cubes

1 cup cherry tomatoes, halved

½ cup sliced Persian cucumber (about ⅛-inch coins)

¼ cup julienned or very thinly sliced red onions

4 tostada shells

1 avocado, pitted, peeled, and very thinly sliced

3 tablespoons furikake

Salsa del Valle (page 133) for garnishing

¼ cup minced chives

In a small mixing bowl, combine the miso, soy sauce, yuzu juice, and olive oil and whisk until blended. Set aside.

In a large mixing bowl, combine the salmon, cherry tomatoes, cucumber, and red onions. Add the miso mixture and toss to coat.

Cover the tostada shells with a layer of sliced avocado. Evenly divvy up the salmon mixture among the tostadas and garnish with the furikake, salsa, and chives. Serve immediately.

FRIED CHICKEN TORTA

We did a party once and had, like, twenty leftover chicken thighs. And so I said, why not do some fried chicken and put it on a torta? I heard somewhere that good fried chicken has eleven herbs and spices, so we experimented a bit and this is what we came up with. Parsley adds a little herbaciousness, but nothing strong like oregano. If you go to most *carnicerias* (butcher shops) here in L.A., the chicken is always bright orange, and that's from the turmeric. Turmeric also breaks down the chicken a bit and tenderizes it. I'd say that makes it even better than KFC.

To make the aïoli 1.0: In a blender, combine the mustard, egg yolk, garlic, lemon juice, Worcestershire, Tabasco, anchovies, and red wine vinegar and blend on medium-high speed until completely mixed. Slowly incorporate the vegetable oil. Take your time—as if you're pouring one out for your homies. Turn to medium speed and blend until the mixture is emulsified but thinner than mayonnaise. Season with more lemon juice or Tabasco, if you like. Transfer to an airtight container and keep in the fridge for up to 1 week.

To make the chipotle crema: In a food processor, combine the sour cream, aïoli, chipotle in adobo, and habanero and process until completely blended. Transfer to an airtight container and store in the fridge for up to 1 week.

In a large bowl, combine the flour, onion powder, garlic powder, cayenne, turmeric, dried parsley, 1 tablespoon salt, and the pepper and stir to mix. Pour the buttermilk into a second bowl. In a 12-inch cast-iron skillet, pour enough vegetable oil to come three-fourths the way up the chicken and heat to 325°F.

Dredge the chicken in the flour mixture, then in the buttermilk.

Add the chicken to the skillet (and if you need to, a little more oil) and fry until golden brown, about 5 minutes. Flip over and fry the other side an additional 3 minutes. Set aside. (Discard the frying oil by placing it in a used coffee can.)

continued

Aïoli 1.0

1 tablespoon Dijon mustard

1 egg yolk

1 garlic clove

Juice of ½ lemon, or as needed

7 dashes Worcestershire sauce

3 dashes Tabasco sauce, or as needed

2 white anchovies

2 tablespoons red wine vinegar

1 cup vegetable oil

Chipotle Crema

1½ cups sour cream

1½ cups Aïoli 1.0 (see above)

2 tablespoons chipotle in adobo

1 habanero chile, stemmed

2 cups all-purpose flour

1 tablespoon onion powder

1 tablespoon garlic powder

1 teaspoon cayenne pepper

1 teaspoon powdered turmeric

1 tablespoon dried parsley

Kosher salt

1½ teaspoons freshly ground black pepper

1 pint buttermilk

Vegetable oil for frying, plus 1 tablespoon

2 boneless skinless chicken thighs

1 large heirloom or beefsteak tomato, sliced ½ inch thick

1 thyme sprig

2 cups arugula

2 tablespoons extra-virgin olive oil

1 tablespoon sherry vinegar

¼ cup fresh flat-leaf parsley leaves, torn from stems

2 tablespoons very thinly sliced red onion

4 ounces aged cheddar, sliced about ¼ inch thick

2 torta buns or bolillos, halved and toasted

Roasted Tomato Salsa (page 139) for garnishing

Season the tomato slices with salt. In the same cast-iron skillet, over high heat, warm the 1 tablespoon vegetable oil. Add the tomatoes and thyme and sear for 1½ to 2 minutes on each side. Transfer to a plate and set aside.

In a large bowl, combine the arugula, olive oil, vinegar, torn parsley, onion, and a pinch of salt. Set aside.

Place two thick slices cheddar on one side of each bun. Spread 2 tablespoons aïoli on the other side. Then place the chicken on top, and garnish with salsa, arugula, and tomato. Serve immediately.

CHILAQUILES TORTA

After going to La Central de Abasto Market in Mexico City, my business partner, Brittney, and I decided to try this cart that had a huge line of people the day before. The chilaquiles torta I had was so delicious and filling that I had to re-create it at Guerrilla Tacos. They offered it with both a green and a red sauce, but I preferred the red so that is the version I've included here. This recipe is best for Sunday mornings, especially when you've been drinking too much mezcal the night before. *Buen provecho.*

In a 10-inch cast-iron skillet over medium-high heat, warm the corn oil to 365°F. Test with a tortilla wedge; it should fry to golden brown in about 2 minutes. Add the tortilla wedges in batches and fry until golden brown. As you remove them from the frying oil, put the chips on metal rack to drain. Lightly season with salt immediately. Pour off all but 2 tablespoons of the oil from the pan.

Return the skillet to medium-high heat. Add all the chiles and toast until they're aromatic, about 1 minute. Add the water, tomatoes, garlic, cumin, and 1 teaspoon salt and cook until the tomatoes are soft. Transfer the contents of the skillet to a blender and blend on high speed. Add the vinegar and season with salt. Set aside.

In a large cast-iron skillet over medium-high heat, add as many chips as will fit and a proportional amount of the tomato mixture and cook until the chips have absorbed the mixture. Keep adding chips and tomato mixture to incorporate. We want the chips moist and slightly mushy. Taste and season with salt, very liberally, and black pepper. These are the chilaquiles; set aside.

In a 10-inch cast-iron skillet over medium heat, combine the butter and onion. Cook until the onion is translucent, about 3 minutes, and then add the Swiss chard. Cook for another 3 minutes. Season with salt. Remove from the heat and set aside.

8 cups corn oil

1 pack (about 60) 5-inch corn tortillas, cut into eighths, like a pizza

Kosher salt

7 guajillo chiles, stemmed and seeded

2 dried California chiles, stemmed and seeded

1 dried ancho chile, stemmed and seeded

2 tablespoons water

8 Roma tomatoes, cored and halved lengthwise

4 garlic cloves, peeled and very thinly sliced

1 tablespoon ground cumin

½ cup white vinegar

Freshly ground black pepper

1 tablespoon unsalted butter

½ white onion, diced

6 cups torn Swiss chard leaves, ribs discarded

continued

One 16-ounce can black beans with about half their liquid

Unsalted butter for frying

6 eggs

6 torta buns or bolillos

Chipotle Crema (page 245) for spreading

1 pound Oaxacan cheese, shredded or torn into chunks

3 avocados, pitted, peeled, quartered, and very thinly sliced

Put the black beans and their liquid in a blender. Puree until they're spreadable, or about the consistency of hummus. Transfer to a pot over low heat, season with salt, and keep warm until you're ready to serve.

In a medium frying pan over medium heat, melt some butter. Add the eggs and fry sunny-side up.

Slice the buns in half and scoop out excess bread from the center so it creates a pocket. Lightly fry the buns with a little bit of butter and salt. Spread the crema on the top slices of the buns. Spread the black bean puree on the bottom slices and scoop some Swiss chard on top. Then add cheese, chilequiles, and a fried egg on top with one half of an avocado. Put the top bun "lids" back on and wrap the tortas with foil so they are easier to handle. Cut in halves, if needed, but most likely you're not going to want to share. Serve immediately.

STREET TATERS

Street taters came about once we got the food truck and had access to a deep-fryer. I've always enjoyed twice-cooked potatoes—essentially french fries. I knew salmon would be good with a lemon crema and the crema would be good with red pepper escabeche. Basically, this is fried potatoes and some condiments you'll find throughout this book.

Prepare an ice-water bath in the largest mixing bowl you have by stirring together water and a tray of ice.

Cut the potatoes lengthwise into sixths or eighths. Put the potatoes in the ice-water bath and let rest for 5 or 6 minutes. Shake the bowl lightly to agitate the water. You should see a billow of cloudy starch coming off. Rinse the potatoes again to remove the starch totally.

In a large stockpot, combine the potatoes with enough cold water to cover. Add salt until it's as salty as the sea. Set over high heat and bring to a boil, then lower the heat to a simmer and cook until the potatoes are very very soft and a knife pierces them super-easily, about 9 minutes. Drain the liquid and put the potatoes in a hotel pan with a rack or somewhere where all the excess water can drip off. After the potatoes are drained and slightly cooled, pop them into the freezer, uncovered, for about a half hour. You don't need them frozen, just cool. It helps them fry.

In a deep-fryer or a pot large enough to deep-fry in, add the rice bran oil—enough to totally cover the potatoes—and bring to 360°F. Add the potatoes, in two batches if you need to, and deep-fry them until golden brown, about 6 minutes. Remove them from the oil and let drain on the same rack you used earlier. Season with salt immediately after they come out of the fryer.

Plate the taters in four bowls, add the salmon, and top with crema, salsa, escabeche, and chives. Serve immediately.

2 pounds potatoes (preferably Kennebec a.k.a. fryer potatoes, or russets)

Kosher salt

4 quarts rice bran oil

8 ounces smoked salmon, chopped into 1-by-1-inch pieces

Lemon Crema (page 38) for topping

Arbol Salsa (page 34) for topping

Red Pepper Escabeche (page 51) for topping

½ cup minced fresh chives or torn parsley

AGUA FRESCA

This is something you do with whatever fresh fruit is seasonal and plentiful. I recommend using berries, or something that's relatively firm, like watermelon, papaya, pineapple, orange, strawberry . . . those are all great. And, of course, you can even get crazy stuff here in California. I once did a white peach with Bill's Bees honey—he does wildflower honey and orange blossom honey—that was super-delicious. Depending on how sweet the fruit is, you can balance it with simple syrup and fresh lime juice, and serve over ice. A lot of the more tropical fruit aguas go very well with rum. With any fruit you'd eat the skins of, like peaches, leave the skins on. Orange makes fucking good agua fresca, but never with the skins.

Add water to this if you want, but typically the ice will melt a bit and dilute it, and it all magically works out.

Simple Syrup

1½ cups sugar

1½ cups water

8 cups rough-cut firm, seasonal fruit, peeled if needed, or berries

8 cups ice cubes, plus more for serving

4 cups water

½ cup fresh lime juice, or to taste

Rum for serving (optional)

To make the simple syrup: In a saucepan over medium heat, combine the sugar and water, bring to a simmer, and whisk until the sugar is dissolved. Turn off the heat and let cool to room temperature. The syrup will keep in an airtight container in the fridge for up to 1 week.

In a Vitamix or blender, puree the fruit on high speed. Put the puree into a 6-quart container.

Add the ice to the puree, and then the simple syrup; mixing it in with a ladle. (Ideally, you want to add the simple syrup when it's room temperature, but if you're in a rush, pour it over the ice when it's still warm so that it cools and does not cook the fruit. That's gross.) Add the water next. Have a taste. Is it too sweet? Add the lime juice until it's not too sweet. Need or want acid? Add more lime juice.

Fill glasses with ice, and pour the agua fresca over that. Add rum, if you like. Serve immediately.

PANTRY STUFF

Here is the key tool and some of the ingredients that made it possible to start Guerrilla Tacos out of a home kitchen in Glendale, California, in 2012. Ninety percent of the cooking is done with these.

Cast-Iron Skillet

You'll be using this in every single recipe in this book. Nowadays these are expensive. They used to be cheaper. It's always best to get them second-hand at a flea market or second-hand store. You'll pay a quarter of what you would new. And at that price, you should have a full set—an assortment anywhere from 6 inches to 12 inches in diameter.

When you get the skillet home, the first thing you should do, especially if you got it at a flea market, is wash it really thoroughly with hot soapy water and a Brillo pad to scrape off any rust. Crank up your oven to 375°F. Dip a thick kitchen towel into a bowl filled with a generous amount of vegetable oil. Use this to oil up the skillet, all over, inside and out. Put the skillet in the oven for an hour. Take the skillet out and baste it again with the oily towel. Be careful because it will be scorching hot. Pop it in for a second hour. Then remove it, let it cool, wipe it down with a clean towel, and put it away. Between uses, just wipe it out with a clean towel. You shouldn't have to wash it every time. When you have gunk building up, repeat the process as described. When it's really, really well-seasoned, you can kind of gently wash it with soap and water.

Butter

All the recipes in this book call for unsalted butter. Here in Southern California, I like to use Plugra. If I can't find Plugra, I like to use Challenge. If you can't find Challenge, just find some nice pure, unsalted butter. My favorite butter in the whole world—to eat with tortillas or bread or waffles—is Beurre de Baratte.

Chile de Árbol

One of the most common chiles found in my household growing up was chile de árbol. You'll find this in many recipes throughout the book. It should be common practice to stem these. We never use stems in any of our preparations. These chiles can be found fresh, but that's pretty rare. Most of the time you find them dry, which is how we use them. Take note that when you roast these in your house, make sure you have pretty good ventilation because sometimes people start coughing. The scent of chiles de árbol roasting will forever remind me of coming home from middle school to find my mom cooking something at the stove.

Lard

If you can't find lard in the butcher's section of your market, go to a Mexican market or a *carniceria* (butcher shop). When buying from a Mexican market, you'll often find lard just sitting out in pint- or quart-size containers. Just pop that in the fridge until you're ready to use. If you can't get to a Mexican market near you, you can always order lard online.

Olive Oil

I like to use cold-pressed extra-virgin olive oil. I typically use local California olive oil if I can find it because I know where it's coming from. For a finishing olive oil, I like Spanish stuff. Any extra-virgin olive oil from Spain should be good for this purpose. If you're in L.A., and shopping at Super King, Al Wazir is a good brand for using in aguachiles and the like.

Salt

For regular everyday cooking I like to use Diamond Crystal Kosher Salt. If you can't find Diamond, Morton's Kosher Salt will do in a pinch. For finishing salt, I like to use fleur de sel or Maldon for seasoning at the end. For tostadas, this is an excellent choice.

Thyme

Whenever I'm referencing thyme in the book, I am always talking about fresh thyme. I never use dry thyme. Fresh thyme you can find anywhere. If you can't find it, grow it yourself!

A NOTE ABOUT SALSAS

Oftentimes in making these recipes, you'll end up with leftover salsa. That's a good thing! You can use any of our salsas as a condiment for eggs or sandwiches—or just look at when other recipes in the book call for a particular salsa as a way of starting a menu for your next Guerrilla Tacos meal.

ACKNOWLEDGMENTS

Thank you to Tanya, a.k.a. MERMER, for holding it down at home, taking care of Pono, and helping me get this crazy thing started. You are my constant, and none of this would be possible without you.

To my mother, who always had the highest expectations for me. And to my dad, Chubbs, for showing me that hard work pays off, that raising a family as an immigrant in this country is possible, and for living the American Dream.

To my brother, Jose, and my sister, Judy, for offering unwavering support of my cooking and Guerrilla Tacos.

To my friend and partner Brittney, who helped me grow the business and taught me a lot along the way. You basically made the dream of a brick-and-mortar a reality. I couldn't have done this without your dedication, patience, love of the industry, and people skills. Thank you.

To the staff at Guerrilla Tacos, present and past.

To the chefs who have been major influences in my career. To Walter Manzke, for teaching me how to peel vegetables. To Gary Menes, for teaching me the importance of ingredient quality and stamina in the kitchen. To Milan Pawar, for letting me experiment on the members of the country club with all my specials. And to all my aunts on the Ponce and the Avila sides for being an endless stream of inspiration.

Thank you to the Ten Speed crew. Nicole, thank you for getting this marriage arranged. You all have been a pleasure to work with.

To Dylan + Jeni, for killing it with the pictures. And thank you for having me in your home and letting me stink up your place with chorizo.

To my venders and suppliers. To Kawai at Luxe Seafood, for selling to me even before I had a license to operate. To Segolene and the crew at Gourmet Imports, thank you darlings! To Stephanie, thanks for all your hard work and for fishing some of the best seafood I've ever seen. To Kris Cook, thanks for meeting me off the 210 and the 2 and in the back streets of Silver Lake to drop off pork. I appreciate and respect all the work you do.

Shout out to the L.A. chefs who have been supporting me as a friend and as a colleague. Sara Kenas, John Butler, Varton Abgaryan, Katsuji Tanabe—for your shit-talking with your little sausage fingers, thanks for the support!—Octavio Olivas, Esdras Ochoa, Ray Garcia, Carlos Delgado and crew, and all the chefs involved with Taste of Mexico.

And to the chef homies on the other side of the border: Diego Hernandez, Enrique Olvera, Lalo Garcia. To Checo and the Boca Negra/Monterrey clique. Thanks for the support, you guys are the shit.

Thank you Handsome Coffee Roasters, Cafe Dulce Pop Up, Cognoscenti Coffee, and Blue Bottle Coffee, for letting me set up my cart before we even had an idea of what the fuck we wanted to do. And to the crew at Silverlake Wine, you guys are also the shit.

To the sucias and maniacs, friends and family, for coming out and eating my tacos.

To my co-author RP3, you've been a heroic collaborator and become a true friend along the way—I'd trust you with anything, including writing this sentence yourself on our deadline day, after noticing I omitted you from my acknowledgments and deciding unilaterally to right that wrong.

Pono, you can't read this, but "Bark-bark-bark, bark. Bark-bark. *I love you. Daddy.*"

And to Talulah, may you rest in peace. The image of chopped cauliflower falling in your golden hair will forever be burned into my memory.

—W.A.

My utmost gratitude to the entire Avila family, for trusting me with this deeply personal story.

To my parents, for giving me my love of food and cooking.

Wes, thank you for believing in my ideas even when they didn't make a lot of sense to you, for letting your guard down and trusting me with your voice (more than you might have known), and for teaching me how to peel vegetables.

Thank you to all at Ten Speed—especially Jenny Wapner, for recommending me for this work and for your patience and guidance throughout, and Emma Campion, for responding to my design mock-ups with such good humor, and to Kelly Snowden and Serena Sigona.

Thank you Brittney Valles, for dealing with me dealing with writing a cookbook with Wes. And to all Guerrilla Tacos staff, thanks for making me feel welcome on the truck.

Nicole Tourtelot, you kicked this thing off and hung tough throughout, even when the razor clams started to move—impressive work.

To my dear friend (and agent) Rebecca Friedman.

To Tanya, thank you for sharing Wes with me.

Dylan + Jeni, please adopt me.

And to Caitlin Esch, without your unwavering support, sharp editorial advice, and nonstop no-nonsense-ness, I couldn't do this, or anything else . . . except maybe cook you dinner. Thank you.

—R.P.

The authors gratefully acknowledge the work of those who tested recipes: Paola Briseño, Nicole Tourtelot, Susan Tourtelot, Rob and Emma Tourtelot, Robert and Lucy Donnelly, Jennifer Preissel, and the Inland Empire Foodies—Dale Mueller, Leo Smith, Amy Montevaldo, Rebecca Hoggarth, Vera Kratochwill, Linda Pililian, Yvonne Serrato, and Paul Montgomery.

INDEX

Some of the recipes in this book include raw eggs, meat, or fish. When these foods are consumed raw, there is always the risk that bacteria, which is killed by proper cooking, may be present. For this reason, when serving these foods raw, always buy certified salmonella-free eggs and the freshest meat and fish available from a reliable grocer, storing them in the refrigerator until they are served. Because of the health risks associated with the consumption of bacteria that can be present in raw eggs, meat, and fish, these foods should not be consumed by infants, small children, pregnant women, the elderly, or any persons who may be immunocompromised. The author and publisher expressly disclaim responsibility for any adverse effects that may result from the use or application of the recipes and information contained in this book.

Copyright © 2017 by Wesley Avila
Photographs copyright © 2017 by Dylan James Ho and Jeni Afuso
Illustrations copyright © 2017 Michael Hirshon

All rights reserved.
Published in the United States by Ten Speed Press, an imprint of the
Crown Publishing Group, a division of Penguin Random House LLC, New York.
www.crownpublishing.com
www.tenspeed.com

Ten Speed Press and the Ten Speed Press colophon are registered
trademarks of Penguin Random House LLC.

Library of Congress Cataloging-in-Publication Data is on file with the publisher.

Hardcover ISBN: 978-0-399-57863-2
eBook ISBN: 978-0-399-57864-9

Printed in China

Design by Emma Campion
Cover Graffiti by Vyal Reyes

10 9 8 7 6 5 4